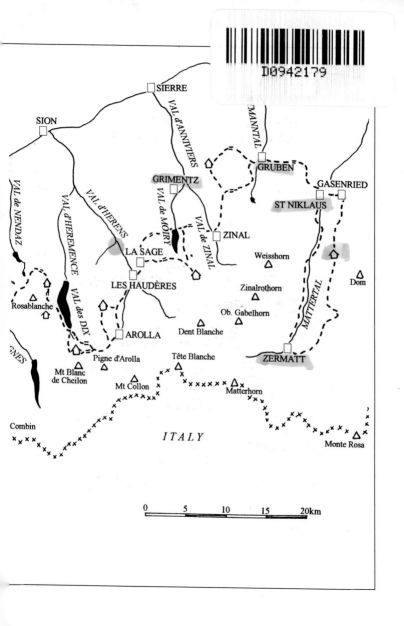

SIERRE

SION

VAL d'ANNIVIERS

MANNTAL

GRUBEN

GASENRIED

GRIMENTZ

ST NIKLAUS

VAL de MOIRY

VAL d'HERENS

VAL de ZINAL

ZINAL

LA SAGE

Weisshorn

VAL de NENDAZ

VAL d'HEREMENCE

LES HAUDÈRES

Zinalrothorn

MATTERTAL

Dom

Rosablanche

VAL des DIX

Ob. Gabelhorn

AROLLA

Dent Blanche

Pigne d'Arolla

Tête Blanche

ZERMATT

GNES

Mt Blanc
de Cheilon

Mt Collon

Matterhorn

Combin

ITALY

Monte Rosa

0   5   10   15   20km

Path junction on the way to Cabane du Mont Fort (Stage 5)

CHAMONIX TO ZERMATT

'The Walker's Haute Route'

Warning note

Every mountain walk has its dangers, and the one described in this guidebook is no exception. All who tackle the Chamonix to Zermatt Walker's Haute Route should recognise this and take responsibility for themselves and their companions along the way. The author and publisher have made every effort to ensure that the information contained herein was correct when the guide went to press, but they cannot accept responsibility for any loss, injury or inconvenience sustained by any person using this book.

International Distress Signal
(To be used in emergency only)
Six blasts on a whistle (and flashes with a torch after dark) spaced evenly for one minute, followed by a minute's pause. Repeat until an answer is received. The response is three signals per minute followed by a minute's pause.

The following signals are used to communicate with a helicopter:

Help needed:
raise both arms above head to form a 'V'

Help not required:
raise one arm above head, extend other arm downward

Note: mountain rescue can be very expensive – be adequately insured

CHAMONIX TO ZERMATT
'The Walker's Haute Route'

by

KEV REYNOLDS

2 POLICE SQUARE, MILNTHORPE
CUMBRIA LA7 7PY
www.cicerone.co.uk

1st Edition 1991
2nd Edition 1995, reprinted 2000
3rd Edition 2001, reprinted 2002

DEDICATION

For my wife – without whose love and practical support this guide-book would not have been written.

ACKNOWLEDGEMENTS

My thanks to Heidi Reisz, Roland Minder and Russell Palmer of the Swiss National Tourist Office for much-appreciated assistance during research for this book; to Daniel Bruchez, guardian of Cabane du Mont Fort for his advice and friendship; and to Hedy and Marcel Füx-Pollinger whose charm, warmth and hospitality in Jungen has been carried on by their successors at the Junger-Stübli, Marcelline and Erich Gruber, whom I am now proud to count among my friends. The guardians at Cabane de Prafleuri, Cabane de Moiry and the Europa Hut have also added much to the pleasures of the route. James Roberts provided information during initial research; I am grateful to him, and to Sîan Pritchard-Jones and Bob Gibbons who suggested the crossing of Col du Tsaté for this third edition. A special note of gratitude is due to my old trekking partner Alan Payne for his company when we first worked out the route, and to my wife who has now trekked it with me twice. Thanks, too, to all those who have written with updates and suggestions, among them: David Angell, Michael Bromfield, James Bruton, John Castle, Richard and Elaine Clare, Tim Ford, R Glaister, Andrew Harper, Keith and Kathy Howard, David Hughes, Ron King, Peter Lewis, Jolanda and Marcel Locher, Jenny Morgan, Bill Orme, Jane Linz Roberts, Ron Roweth, Michael and Billie Strauss, David Whewell – with apologies to any left out whose names I could not decipher. And finally, I am thankful as ever for the continued backing of my publishers, who provide so many excuses to spend long weeks of delight in the Alps and elsewhere.

Kev Reynolds

Front cover: The Dom and Ried glacier from the classic Twära viewpoint

KEV REYNOLDS

KEV REYNOLDS, author of this guide, is a freelance writer, photojournalist and lecturer whose first title for Cicerone Press (*Walks & Climbs in the Pyrenees*) appeared in 1978, and is still in print. He has published many books on the Alps, a series of trekkers' guides to the Nepal Himalaya and, nearer to home, several on walking in Southern England. The first Honorary Member of the British Association of European Mountain Leaders, member of the Alpine Club, Austrian Alpine Club and Outdoor Writers' Guild, Kev's enthusiasm for mountains in particular, and the countryside in general, remains undiminished after 40 years of activity. Living among what he calls the 'Kentish Alps' he regularly travels throughout Britain to share that enthusiasm through his lectures.

Alpine guides by the same author published by Cicerone Press:

Alpine Pass Route
Walks in the Engadine – Switzerland
Tour of the Vanoise
The Valais
The Jura (with R B Evans)
The Bernese Alps
Ticino
Central Switzerland
Écrins National Park
100 Hut Walks in the Alps
Walking in the Alps

CONTENTS

Appendices

ROUTE PROFILE KEY

 accommodation: hotel, dortoir, youth hostel, mountain hut

 Official campsite

 Refreshments: food and/or drinks

 Bus service

 Railway station

 Cable car

 Gondola lift

3 hrs 45 mins | Walking time from start of stage

All heights in metres

PREFACE TO THE THIRD EDITION

Since the second edition of *Chamonix to Zermatt* was published a few minor changes have occurred to the original route, as well as the creation of an exciting high path along the east flank of the Mattertal which provides a more dramatic and scenically spectacular approach to Zermatt than was hitherto possible. This is a good opportunity to incorporate these changes into the guide, and to make what was already a tremendous walk even better.

A more rewarding first stage to Argentière has been worked out which gives superb views of the Drus and the Chamonix aiguilles, and a few alternative options are offered elsewhere, including a direct crossing on Stage 9 between La Sage and Cabane de Moiry. One of the most significant changes to the original route has been caused by glacial shrinkage. On Stage 6 it is no longer advisable to cross the Grand Désert glacier. Instead one must descend below it, pass round a glacial lake and then ascend a stony slope to rejoin the 'old' way to Col de Prafleuri. This adds about 30 minutes to what was already a fairly long day's walk, but should be welcomed by trekkers who were previously nervous about this glacier crossing.

Several additions to the accommodation lists have been included, and I've brought up to date telephone numbers that were unfortunately changed a few months after the second edition was published. Facilities at the few mountain huts used along the way have been improved, and by the time the present guide is out a long-overdue new Cabane de Prafleuri will have been opened, and work should have begun on extending and refurbishing Cabane du Mont Fort.

What has not changed is the beauty of the mountains and the charm of the valleys. Glaciers may shrivel, rockfall rearrange a small section of mountainside, lakes grow in extent or shrink around their edges; but the scenic rewards of the Chamonix to Zermatt Walker's Haute Route are every bit as powerful as they ever were. It's a fabulous route across an amazing series of landscapes.

May you find as much pleasure on your journies as I have on mine.

Kev Reynolds

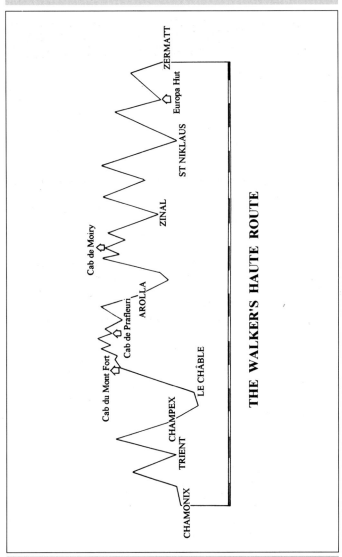

THE WALKER'S HAUTE ROUTE

CHAMONIX

TRIENT

CHAMPEX

LE CHÂBLE

Cab du Mont Fort

Cab de Prafleuri

AROLLA

Cab de Moiry

ZINAL

ST NIKLAUS

Europa Hut

ZERMATT

INTRODUCTION

CHAMONIX TO ZERMATT, Mont Blanc to the Matterhorn. What pictures these names conjure in the minds of those of us who love mountains! The two greatest mountaineering centres in the world; one overshadowed by the highest massif in Western Europe and the other by the most famous, if not the most elegant and most instantly recognised, of all mountains.

Chamonix to Zermatt, Mont Blanc to the Matterhorn – recipe for a visual feast!

To walk from one to the other is to sample that feast in full measure; a gourmet extravaganza of scenic wonders from first day till last and each one (to carry the metaphor to its limit) a course that both satisfies and teases the palate for more.

The Walker's Haute Route does just that.

In two weeks of mountain travel you will be witness to the greatest collection of four thousand metre peaks in all the Alps and visit some of the most spectacular valleys. There you'll find delightful villages and remote alp hamlets, wander flower meadows and deep fragrant forests, skirt exquisite tarns that toss mountains on their heads, cross icy streams and clamber beside glaciers that hang suspended from huge buttresses of rock. You'll traverse lonely passes and descend into wild, stone-filled corries. There will be marmots among the boulders and ibex on the heights. And your days will be filled with wonder.

The route is over 180 kilometres long. It crosses eleven passes, gains more than twelve thousand metres in height and loses more than ten thousand. And each pass gained is a window onto a world of stunning beauty.

There's the Mont Blanc range and the chain of the Pennine Alps, one massif after another of snowbound glory: Mont Blanc itself, with its organ-pipe aiguilles; the overpowering mass of the Grand Combin; Mont Blanc de Cheilon and Pigne d'Arolla, Mont Collon and Tête Blanche and the huge tooth of Dent Blanche. There's the Grand Cornier, Ober Gabelhorn and Weisshorn and stiletto pointed Zinalrothorn; then there's the Dom and Täschhorn, Breithorn and Matterhorn and all their crowding neighbours sheathed in ice and snow to act as a backcloth to dreams; a background landscape to the Walker's Haute Route, contender for the title of Most Beautiful Walk in Europe.

THE WALKER'S HAUTE ROUTE

THE ORIGINAL High Level Route (*Haute Route*), from Chamonix to Zermatt and beyond, was developed more than a hundred years ago. But this was very much a mountaineer's expedition, for it traced a meandering line among the great peaks of the Pennine Alps by linking a number of glacier passes. James David Forbes, scientist and active mountaineer, pioneered an important section of this in 1842 when he crossed Col d'Hérens, Col de Fenêtre and Col du Mont Collon. Alfred Wills also made early explorations, but it was mainly a joint effort by other members of the Alpine Club, notably J F Hardy, William Mathews, Francis Fox Tuckett, F W Jacomb and Stephen Winkworth and their guides, that saw a complete High Level Route established in 1861. This route went from Chamonix to Col d'Argentière, then via Val Ferret, Orsières, Bourg St Pierre, Col de Sonadon, Col d'Oren, Praraye, Col de Valpelline and on to Zermatt.

The following year (1862) Col des Planards was discovered, which led to Orsières being by-passed, thereby allowing a better line to be made in the link between the northern edge of the Mont Blanc range and that of the Pennine Alps.

This High Level Route was, of course, primarily a summer mountaineering expedition that was no small undertaking, especially when one considers the fact that at the time there were no mountain huts as we know them now and all supplies had to be carried a very long way. But with the introduction of skis to the Alps in the late nineteenth century a new concept in winter travel became apparent, and with the first important ski tour being made in the Bernese Alps in 1897, and the subsequent winter ascent of major mountains aided by ski (Monte Rosa in 1898, Breithorn 1899, Strahlhorn 1901, etc), it was clearly only a matter of time before the challenge of the High Level Route would be subjected to winter assault.

In 1903 the first attempt was made to create a ski traverse of the Pennine Alps, and although this and other attempts failed, in January 1911 Roget, Kurz, Murisier, the brothers Crettex and Louis Theytaz succeeded in establishing a winter route from Bourg St Pierre to Zermatt.

Having successfully hijacked the original High Level Route as the ski-touring route *par excellence*, and having translated its British title

From the Europaweg high above Täsch, a fine view of the Matterhorn entices the walker

as the *Haute Route*, the journey from Chamonix to Zermatt came to be seen almost universally as a winter (or more properly, a spring) expedition; a true classic that is, understandably, the focus of ambition for many experienced skiers and ski-mountaineers today.

But there's another Chamonix to Zermatt high level route that is very much a classic of its kind; a walker's route that never quite reaches three thousand metres on any of its passes, that requires no technical mountaineering skills to achieve, avoids glacier crossings and yet rewards with some of the most dramatic high mountain views imaginable.

This is the Chamonix to Zermatt Walker's Haute Route.

It leads comfortably from the base of Mont Blanc to the Swiss frontier at Col de Balme, and from there down to Trient following the route of the Tour of Mont Blanc or one of its *variantes*. The next pass is Fenêtre d'Arpette leading to Champex, and from there down to the junction of Val d'Entremont and Val de Bagnes, then curving round the foot of the mountains to Le Châble. Avoiding Verbier a steep climb brings you to Cabane du Mont Fort, and continues high above the valley heading south-east before crossing three cols in quick succession in order to pass round the northern flanks of Rosablanche.

From Cabane de Prafleuri the route heads over Col des Roux and along the shores of Lac des Dix, then on to Arolla by one of two ways: Col de Riedmatten or the neighbouring Pas de Chèvres via Cabane des Dix. Arolla leads to Les Haudères and up to La Sage on a green hillside above Val d'Hérens in readiness for tackling Col du Tsaté. This rocky col gives access to Val de Moiry and its hut perched in full view of a tremendous icefall, and from where the crossing of Col de Sorebois takes the walker into Val de Zinal, the upper reaches of the glorious Val d'Anniviers. From Zinal to Gruben in the Turtmanntal the route goes either by way of Hotel Weisshorn and the Meidpass or by the more direct Forcletta, and from Gruben a final climb to the ancient crossing point of the Augstbordpass leads to the Mattertal. A long but easy valley walk to Zermatt is the basic final stage, but a two-day alternative and much better option now adopts the dramatic Europaweg which makes a true high-level traverse of the east wall of the valley, with an overnight stay in the Europa Hut.

Every stage has its own special attributes, its own unique splendour, and all add up to a walk of classic proportions. It is, of course, a scenic extravaganza whose main features are the mountains that form the landscapes through which you walk.

First of these is dominated by the Mont Blanc massif with its towering aiguilles creating stark outlines against a backwash of snow and ice. Unbelievably high and seemingly remote from valley-based existence, the dome of the Monarch of the Alps glows of an evening, shines under a midday sun and imposes itself on panoramas viewed from cols several days' walk from the crowded boulevards of Chamonix.

Then there's the Grand Combin making a fair imitation of its loftier neighbour as it swells above the deep cut of Val de Bagnes. This too is a vast mountain whose presence is felt many days' walk away, a grand block of glacial artistry that lures and entices from afar.

Heading round Rosablanche gives a taste of the other side of the mountain world, where gaunt screes and dying glaciers contrast the gleaming snows of its upper slopes. But then Mont Blanc de Cheilon returns the eye to grandeur on an epic scale, with Pigne d'Arolla and

Mont Collon adding their handsome profiles for close inspection, while far off a first brief glimpse of the Matterhorn promises much for the future.

Val de Moiry holds many surprises with its tarns, dammed lake, majestic icefall and contorted glaciers, while Col de Sorebois and all the way down to Zinal is one long adoration of the Weisshorn. The head of Val de Zinal is so magnificent that one yearns to be able to explore further, but the route northward denies that opportunity yet still allows it to be seen in true perspective – a fabulous cirque giving birth to glaciers that have carved a valley of much loveliness.

The Turtmanntal takes you back a hundred years and more. Above it once more rises the Weisshorn, along with Tête de Milon, Bishorn and Brunegghorn and a caliper of glaciers spilling into the valley.

One of the finest viewpoints of the whole walk comes an hour and a half below the Augstbordpass between Turtmanntal and Mattertal. The Mattertal is a long green shaft a thousand metres below. Across the valley shines the Dom with the tongue-like Riedgletscher hanging from it. Above to the right is the Brunegghorn with the Weisshorn beyond, while at the head of the valley is seen that great snowy mass which runs between Monte Rosa and the Matterhorn. But the Matterhorn itself keeps you waiting. Cross the valley at St Niklaus and climb steeply to Gasenried, then walk the length of the Europaweg and you'll not only have the Bishorn and Weisshorn (yet again), but also the Schalihorn, Pointe Sud de Moming and Zinalrothorn, and the incomparable Matterhorn at last seen as it should be seen, from its roots above Zermatt to its cocked-head summit nearly three thousand metres above the valley. It's a view worth waiting for. A view worth walking all the way from Chamonix to savour.

Despite its high passes, despite the fact that it runs across the grain of the country where deep valleys slice between the long outstretched arms of some of the highest mountains in Western Europe, the Chamonix to Zermatt route is not the sole preserve of the hardened mountain walker – although there are some taxing stages and a few delicate exposed sections that might give an understandable twinge of concern to first-time wanderers among the Alps. Most days lead into a touch of 'civilisation', albeit sometimes this civilisation might be just a small mountain village with few amenities. Every night there will be a lodging place with the possibility of meals provided, thereby making it unnecessary to carry camping or cooking equipment. Backpacking on this route is a choice, not an obligation.

Lodgings on the Walker's Haute Route are in themselves very much a part of the mountain experience. In villages they allow you to capture some of the region's culture. In remote mountain huts the wanderer is introduced to the climber's world, with an opportunity to witness high alpine scenes that are normally privy only to the mountaineer.

These lodgings vary from hotels (there are luxuriously-appointed hotels in certain villages on the route for those inclined and financially able to make use of them), to gîtes and basic refuges, and mattresses spread on the floor of communal dormitories in the attic of a pension or inn. But determined campers must understand that organised camp-sites are not to be found in all valleys, and that wild camping is officially discouraged in Switzerland.

Wherever lodgings (and campsites) are to be found along the route mention is made in the text. Similarly, wherever alternative methods of transport occur (train, bus, cable-car, etc), brief details are given. This is to aid any walkers who might fall behind their schedule due to bad weather, unseasonal conditions, sickness or just plain weariness.

The walk outlined in this guide may be achieved within a two-week holiday, while those with plenty of time available are given options which would extend the route and increase the overall experience. These options are outlined below. The longest stage demands 7½ hours of walking, but there are several days of only 4 hours each. Some of the less-demanding days could be amalgamated by fit trekkers in order to reduce the time required to complete the route, should they not have a full fortnight at their disposal, but it would be a pity to do so. This is a walk, above all others, that ought to be wandered at a gentle pace; the very best of mountain holidays.

The first stage (Chamonix to Argentière – 2 hours) may be seen as a prelude. Should you arrive late in the day in Chamonix as you would, for example, if you flew from the U.K. to Geneva and travelled from there by train, then you would probably only have sufficient time to reach Argentière on foot that day. However, if your travel arrangements get you to Chamonix at a reasonable time in the morning (on the overnight train from Paris, for example), it might be feasible to walk all the way to Trient, thus combining two stages for a 7½–8 hour day, thereby cutting a day off the overall route.

Stage 12a (St Niklaus to Gasenried) links the original Haute Route with the new finish along the Europaweg, and takes about 1½ hours walking time. However, it is not really practical to add this short stage to the demanding Augstbordpass crossing (Stage 12), nor tack it on at the start of Stage 13. If you cannot allow a full day for this walk, it is possible to take a bus from St Niklaus to Gasenried itself – either at the end of Stage 12, or first thing on the morning of Stage 13.

One or two commercial trekking companies follow a large portion of the Walker's Haute Route, but opt for public transport over some sections in order to allow a day or two in Zermatt at the end of a two-week holiday. This is an option available to the individual trekker too, of course. But again, it would be a shame to miss any single stage of this route, for each bears witness to the last and forms a unique link with the next.

The Complete Route: 14/15 days

1: Chamonix – Argentière
2: Argentière – Trient
3: Trient – Champex
4: Champex – Le Châble
5: Le Châble – Cab. Mont Fort
6: Mont Fort – Cab. Prafleuri
7: Prafleuri – Arolla
8: Arolla – La Sage
9: La Sage – Cab. de Moiry
10: Moiry – Zinal
11: Zinal – Gruben
12: Gruben – St Niklaus
12a: St Niklaus – Gasenried
     (1½ hrs walk – or bus)
13: Gasenried – Europa Hut
14: Europa Hut – Zermatt

A 12-day Trek

1: Chamonix – Trient
2: Trient – Champex
3: Champex – Le Châble
4: Le Châble – Cab. Mont Fort
5: Mont Fort – Cab. Prafleuri
6: Prafleuri – Arolla
7: Arolla – La Sage
8: La Sage – Cab. de Moiry
9: Moiry – Zinal
10: Zinal – Gruben
11: Gruben – St Niklaus
12: St Niklaus – Zermatt

GETTING THERE AND BACK AGAIN

TRAVEL TO SWITZERLAND is relatively easy. Regular scheduled flights from the U.K. are operated principally by Swissair, its subsidiary Crossair, British Airways and EasyJet.

Geneva is the most convenient airport for reaching Chamonix. Swissair (☎ 020 7434 7300) fly there from London Heathrow. Crossair

(☎ same number as Swissair) operate services from London City, Manchester, Edinburgh and Birmingham. British Airways (☎ 0845 722 2111) fly from London Heathrow and Gatwick, Birmingham and Manchester. EasyJet (☎ 0870 600 0000) have flights from London Gatwick, Luton, Stansted and Liverpool – bookings by telephone or Internet only.

There are currently no direct flights to Geneva from Dublin, but Crossair fly to Zürich with coordinated interconnecting flights from there back to Geneva.

From the USA Swissair operate daily scheduled non-stop flights from New York to Geneva, but it's possible to find interconnecting flights by British Airways via London Heathrow from other cities in the States.

All scheduled flights from Canada at present fly to Zürich – Air Canada fly daily from Toronto, Swissair from Montreal.

Onward travel to Chamonix from Geneva is either by twice-daily bus from the airport, or by train from the airport to Martigny, where you change to the Mont Blanc Express (change again at Le Châtelard on the Swiss/French border).

Travel by rail from the U.K. is straightforward. A superfast London–Paris service is operated by Eurostar (☎ 0345 303030) through the Channel Tunnel, with onward journey to Chamonix.

A low-price alternative worth considering is by Eurolines overnight coach from London (Victoria Coach Station) to Chamonix. Bookings can be made through National Express agents, by telephone (☎ 08705 143219) or via the Internet (www.eurolines.co.uk). Cut-price promotional fares are often available when booked at least 14 days in advance – conditions include return within a month, and no open-dated returns.

Return from Zermatt at the end of the walk will be by train via Visp to Geneva (for flight), to Lausanne (connections for Paris-bound trains) or to Martigny for the Mont Blanc Express route to Chamonix in order to connect with Eurolines return coach to London.

ACCOMMODATION

PRACTICALLY EVERY village along the route of this walk has a wide selection of accommodation and facilities to choose from, while between villages there are often mountain inns of one sort or another where an overnight lodging may be found. In the early stages there are also several *gîtes d'étape* which are very much like privately-owned

Hotel Weisshorn (Alternative Stage 11)

youth hostels, with (usually) low-cost dormitory accommodation and communal washrooms. In addition there are privately-owned mountain huts and others belonging to the Swiss Alpine Club in which non-members can spend a night too.

Outline details are given throughout the text wherever lodgings exist. Telephone numbers are also provided where possible to enable walkers to call ahead to reserve beds – this is especially important during the high season. (Note that if you are calling locally, the initial three digits of the number given in brackets ie: (027) should be ignored.)

It might also be worth noting that the cost of accommodation in Switzerland need not be as prohibitively high as some might fear. Whilst it is pointless quoting specific prices in a guidebook that could be in print for several years, comparisons with U.K. costs are very favourable. Bed and breakfast rates in modest hotels used on this route will be on a par with charges made in British establishments, or even cheaper in many cases. And a good and filling evening meal in a Swiss restaurant need cost no more than a pub meal in the U.K. Half-pension (*demi-pension/halb-pension*) usually provides the most economical deal. Hotel standards are high, and service will be friendly.

Bed and breakfast in private homes (*Chambres d'Hôtes/ Gästezimmer*) is another option worth considering. A booklet containing details of such accommodation within the Valais region is available from : BnB – Chambres d'Hôtes – VS13, Cathy Renggli, Rte des Liddes 12, CH 3960 Sierre, Switzerland; or contact Switzerland Tourism (☎ 020 7734 1921) – addresses given in Appendix C.

In a few villages along the way it may be possible to rent a private room in a furnished chalet for a night. Some of these rooms have self-catering facilities, otherwise you will need to find a restaurant for your meals. A self-contained room can be economically viable, and where such places are known from personal experience, mention is made in the text. Otherwise, enquire at the local tourist office.

Dortoirs (*matratzenlager* in German) are highly recommended for walkers who do not object to a lack of privacy. Some hotels offer *dortoir* accommodation in an attic or an outbuilding, while a few establishments are specifically set-up as privately-run youth hostels – the *gîtes d'étape* mentioned above. In my experience these places offer good value for money. They vary in style, but all provide mixed dormitory accommodation and simple washing facilities. Most have hot showers. Some have individual two-tier bunk beds, others merely offer mattresses on the floor of a large room under the roof. One or two also provide the means for self-catering, whilst the majority offer a full meals service. Those with experience of staying in youth hostels should be more than content with the *dortoirs* on the Chamonix to Zermatt route.

Mountain huts of the Swiss Alpine Club (SAC) are also used on this route – as well as two that are privately owned. Membership of an affiliated alpine club with reciprocal rights will give reduced overnight fees in SAC huts. (If you are a member of the U.K. section of the Austrian Alpine Club, for example, do not forget to take your membership card with you.) Members of the British Mountaineering Council (BMC) can also obtain a reciprocal rights card that is recognised here. (Addresses and contact numbers of both the Austrian Alpine Club and BMC will be found in Appendix C.)

Mountain huts have mixed dormitory accommodation. Most of those visited on this route provide meals and drinks (neither Refuge Les Grands on Alternative Stage 2, nor Refuge de la Gentiane la Barma passed on Stage 7 are permanently manned in summer). Where available, evening meals in huts are invariably filling and high in calorific value. Washroom facilities are sometimes rather basic, and hot water is the exception rather than the rule.

On arrival at a mountain hut remove your boots before entering and help yourself to a pair of hut shoes found on a rack just inside the door. Locate the guardian to book bedspace for the night and put your name down for any meals you may require. There will sometimes be a choice of menu, but not always. Blankets and pillows are provided in the dormitories, but a sheet sleeping bag (sleeping bag liner) is well worth carrying with you for purposes of hygiene. Some of these huts are used by climbers who may need to make a pre-dawn start, and whilst your sleep may well be disturbed by those leaving early, it is important that you do not disturb others if you go to bed after they have settled.

As for camping, officially approved sites are to be found in a number of valleys along the route, but certainly not in all of them. Where they do exist facilities range from adequate to good. Off-site camping is offically discouraged in Switzerland since grasslands form a valuable part of the agricultural economy, and although it would not be beyond the bounds of possibility for individual backpackers to find a discreet corner of an alp for a single night's stay, it would be irresponsible to indicate likely sites in this book. Wherever possible please ask permission of farmers. It has always been my experience in Switzerland that whenever a farmer has been approached, permission has readily been granted and a good site pointed out. In all cases, wherever you camp be discreet, take care not to foul water supplies, light no fires and pack all litter away with you.

Mention of any establishment in this book, whether as an overnight lodging or as a place where refreshments may be had, should not necessarily be taken as an endorsement of services on offer.

WEATHER

DESPITE THE advanced elevation of its mountains the Valais region which our route traverses enjoys some of the best weather conditions of all Switzerland. South of the Rhône valley the average annual precipitation is considerably less than that of the Bernese Oberland, for example, in whose rain-shadow it lies. Summer temperatures are also higher than the altitude might otherwise suggest, with 25°C being not uncommon on windless days in the mountains. However, night-time temperatures can quickly plunge.

When the Föhn winds blow there will be clear skies for days at a time. But in the wake of this warm dry wind, rain should be expected. Snow can fall at any time of the year in the higher valleys and on hill-sides, and in early summer particularly, sudden storms with plenty of lightning are not at all uncommon.

Weather patterns vary from year to year and it is therefore impossible to predict with any certainty the likelihood of arranging a fair-weather holiday. In any case, no-one should head for the mountains and expect unlimited sunshine. Go prepared for rain and be thankful if you have little or none! But there is some comfort in the knowledge that the Pennine Alps of canton Valais receive on average a much better summer than many other alpine regions, with more sunshine, higher temperatures and less rainfall than several neighbouring areas.

July would normally be the earliest time for walkers to consider tackling this route. Before then avalanches and poor snow conditions would effectively prevent the crossing of several passes. Even early July will be too soon in some years – much depends on the amount and timing of the previous winter's snowfall. September is probably the optimum month, with crisp cold nights and bright days with clear skies.

Day to day weather forecasts may be obtained in Switzerland by telephone. The number to dial is 162. Local tourist information offices and guides' bureaux often display a 2–3 day forecast, and sometimes there's a barometer on show by which you can check pressure trends. Up-to-date advice may also be sought from the guardians at mountain huts.

NOTES FOR WALKERS

THOSE WHO tackle the Chamonix to Zermatt route will reap countless rewards. Those rewards will be received at best when you are physically fit and mentally tuned. Crossing the grain of the country means that there will be many steep uphill and downhill sections to face, and since it is important to enjoy every aspect of the first pass as much as the last, fitness should be there from the very beginning.

Taking regular exercise at home will go some way towards conditioning yourself to the physical demands of the route. Of course, the best way to prepare yourself for a mountain walking holiday is by walking. Uphill. Carry a rucksack with a few belongings in it to accustom your shoulders to the weight. If on the first day out from Chamonix your lungs and legs complain, then you've no doubt not done enough to get fit, and the crossing of Col de Balme may be less enjoyable than it deserves.

Mental fitness is as important as the physical, and the two often go hand in hand. If you gaze with dread at the amount of height to be gained in order to cross a pass, no doubt you will suffer in consequence. Let every day be greeted with eagerness. Find joy in the steep uphill as well as the downward slope. Draw strength from the beauty of the scenes around you; enjoy the movement of clouds, the wind and wildness as much as the gleam of sunshine, the raw crags and screes of desolation as well as the lush flower-strewn pastures and distant snowscapes. Each is an integral part of the mountain world; a world of magic and mystery. It's a world through which it is a great privilege to move in freedom. Don't take a moment of this experience for granted.

The choice of equipment is also important. Boots need to be lightweight, comfortable, fit well and be broken-in before heading for the Alps. They should give ankle support and have thick cleated soles (Vibram or similar) that are not worn smooth. You will need as much grip as possible on some sections.

Gaiters are favoured by many British hill walkers who regularly face long wet grass or boggy moorlands at home. In most cases gaiters will not be necessary for this route, although short ankle cuffs (*stop touts*) will help keep small stones and grit out of your boots.

Good waterproofs are essential, not just as protection against rain or snowfall, but to double as windproofs. Jacket and overtrousers made from a 'breathable' material are recommended. Bearing in mind that some of the passes are almost 3000 metres high, a warm pullover or pile jacket should also be taken, as should a woollen hat or balaclava, and gloves.

If one needs to be prepared for the wet and cold, it is also necessary to take preventative action against long periods of extreme sun and unshaded heat. A brimmed sunhat, suncream (Factor 10 or stronger) and sunglasses should be part of your equipment.

A first-aid kit must be included. Waterbottle, compass, headtorch and spare batteries, whistle and maps should also be carried, as should a small amount of emergency food. (This can be recharged regularly as you pass through villages.) A sheet sleeping bag (sleeping bag liner) is highly recommended for use in *dortoirs* and mountain huts. A conventional sleeping bag, however, will not be needed unless you plan to camp. Trekking poles can be invaluable in preventing a lot of discomfort or pain on steep downhill sections.

A well-fitting rucksack with a waist-belt adjusted to take the weight of your pack is important. It need not be very large since you should be able to keep equipment down to ten kilograms (20lbs) at most – unless you plan to backpack with full camping gear, that is. A large thick polythene bag in which to pack all your equipment inside the sack will protect items from getting wet in the event of bad weather – even if you have a waterproof rucksack cover. A selection of plastic bags of assorted sizes will also be useful.

On all but the final two valleys of the walk the route passes through French-speaking territory, but once you cross from Zinal into the Turtmanntal German becomes the official language. Although the non-linguist may have difficulty conversing in general terms with locals met in the mountains, English is widely understood in most of the villages, and you will probably face no real language problems in hotels or other lodgings. The Appendix contains a glossary of French and German words likely to be met along the way, but it is no substitute for either a pocket dictionary or a phrase-book.

PATHS AND WAYMARKS

MOST OF THE paths adopted by this route will have been in use for centuries by farmers, traders and hunters going about their daily business – from alp to alp, or from one valley to the next by way of an ancient pass, or up onto a ridge where chamois or ibex might be spotted. A few will be of recent origin, either laid out by a local commune, by a branch of the Swiss Footpath Protection Association, by the Valais Rambling Association (*Association Valaisanne de la Randonnée Pédestre*) or by members of the SAC in order to reach a mountain hut.

There are two official types of footpath in Switzerland which are signposted and waymarked to a common standard. A *chemin pedestre* (*wanderweg*) is a path that remains either in the valley, or along the hillsides at a modest altitude. These are maintained and graded at a more gentle angle than the *chemin de montagne* or *bergweg*. Yellow

Täschalp (Stage 14)

metal signposts bear the names of major landmark destinations such as a pass, lake, hut or village, often with estimated times given in hours (*Heures* in French, *Stunden* in German-speaking regions) and minutes (*Min*). A white plate on these yellow signs names the immediate locality and, sometimes, the altitude. Along the trail occasional yellow signs or paint flashes on rocks are also found.

A mountain path (*chemin de montagne* or *bergweg*) is one which ventures higher and is more demanding than the *chemin pedestre/wanderweg*. These paths will usually be rougher, narrower, and sometimes fading if not in regular use. Signposting will be similar to that already described, except that the outer sections of the finger post will be painted red and white, and the intermediate paint flashes along the way will be blazed white–red–white. Occasional cairns may also be used to direct the way over boulder slopes, or where poor visibility could create difficulties. In the event of mist or low cloud obscuring the onward route, it is essential to study the area of visibility with the utmost care before venturing on to the next paint flash or stone-built cairn. In extreme cases it may be necessary to take compass bearings and make progress from one to the other in this manner.

Currently the most difficult paths are found on: i] Stage 6 between Col de Louvie and Col de Prafleuri where the route makes a traverse of a large area of rocks and boulders, ii] on the approach to Col de la Chaux on Alternative Stage 6, iii] on the crossing of Col de Riedmatten (Stage 7), and iv] along the Europaweg on the final two stages leading to Zermatt. On this impressive and visually spectacular trail many exposed sections have been safeguarded with fixed rope handrails, and on several occasions the way crosses potentially hazardous areas where rockfall is a concern. Warning signs have been fixed telling walkers to hurry across the danger areas.

SAFETY IN THE MOUNTAINS

WHILST THE ROUTE is mostly well signposted (without ever mentioning the Chamonix to Zermatt Haute Route) with good paths for the majority of the way, and there are working farms and villages at frequent intervals along the route, there are also wild and remote sections where an accident could have serious consequences. It should be recognised that participation in any mountain activity places a need for personal responsibility and self-reliance, for all mountain areas – the Alps as much as any – contain a variety of objective dangers for the unwary, and the long distance walker should be prepared to deal with any hazards that arise.

Plan each day's walk carefully. Study the route outline, the amount of height to be gained and lost, and the time required to reach your destination. None of the stages described are particularly long, but in case you are tempted to double up, make sure you have enough hours of daylight in which to cross the day's pass and descend to the safety of the next valley, or to where a night's lodging may be had before nightfall. Carry a few emergency food rations and a first-aid kit. (It would be sensible to invest in good first-aid training – not just for the C–Z trek, but for everyday emergencies.) Know how to read a map and compass, and watch for signs of deteriorating weather. Never be too proud to turn back if it is safer to do so than to continue in the face of an on-coming storm or on a trail that has become unjustifiably dangerous.

In the unhappy event of an accident, stay calm. Should the party be large enough to send for help whilst someone remains with the injured member, make a careful *written* note of the precise location where the victim can be found. If there is a mountain hut or farm nearby, seek assistance there. If valley habitation is nearer, find a telephone and dial **117** (Police) or **1414** which calls out helicopter rescue (REGA) – **this should be used only if absolutely essential.**

> **The international distress call is a series of six signals (blasts on a whistle and – after dark – flashes with a torch) spaced evenly for a minute, followed by one minute's pause, then repeat with a further six signals. The reply is three signals per minute followed by a minute's pause.**

Note i: There is no free mountain rescue service in Switzerland, and no free hospital treatment. The result of an emergency could therefore be extremely costly. Remember that Switzerland is not a member of the EU so there will be no medical cover available under form E111. Be adequately insured, and be cautious. The addresses of several specialist insurance companies dealing with mountain walking /trekking holidays are given in Appendix C.

Note ii: It is advisable to leave a copy of your travel itinerary and insurance details with a responsible friend or relative at home, and to carry with you photo-copies of important documents – information pages of your passport, insurance certificate, travel tickets, etc – as well as an emergency home contact address and telephone number.

FLORA AND FAUNA

THE PENNINE ALPS contain the richest flora in all Switzerland. One of the factors responsible for this is the mixture of limestone, gneiss and schistose rocks, which encourages calcipile (lime-loving) plants to flourish in some areas, calcifuge varieties in others. Climatic considerations also play an important role, as does the marked difference in altitude between valley bed and the upper plant zone. Walkers who daily cross the high passes in a traverse of the region – particularly in the early summer – will wander through a number of successive plant zones, and one does not have to be a trained botanist to enjoy the variety of flowers and shrubs on show. There are, however, several handy well-illustrated guidebooks available that provide at-a-glance information on specific flowers likely to be seen.

There will be all the expected varieties, from gentian to edelweiss, from alpenrose to crimson-eyed primulas, and many more besides. This is not the place to list them all. Newcomers to the Alps may be surprised to find that it is not only the meadowlands that reward with bloom, but that even the high, seemingly lifeless cliff faces, screes, and glacier-bordering moraines have their own species of flowering plants, and it is often such discoveries that make days in the mountains so memorable.

Of all creatures native to the Alps the one most likely to be seen on this walk is the engaging marmot (*Marmota marmota*). On many days you will no doubt first hear a sharp shrill whistle as you cross a boulder slope or wander a high alp on the borders of grassland and scree. This is the marmot's warning cry, and you may then see two or three brown, furry creatures scurrying for cover.

The marmot is a gregarious animal, living in colonies among a variety of mountain and valley locations in burrows whose entrance holes may be seen from some of the footpaths on the walk. They grow to the size of a large hare and weigh up to ten kilograms (22lbs), hibernating in winter for around five months, then emerging in spring when the snow cover melts. Their young are born during the early summer when you may be lucky enough to catch sight of two or three kitten-sized creatures romping or playfully fighting in the short grass of the upper hillsides.

Chamois (*Rupicapra rupicapra*) are rarely seen at close quarters, but in the high mountain regions just below the snowline, it is not unusual to spy a small herd picking its way with commendable ease over excessively steep terrain. On occasion they can be seen grazing on the forest fringe. From a distance it is possible to mistake chamois, with their small curving horns, for female or young ibex. Ibex, however, have a stockier body.

Ibex (*Capra ibex*) are also known as *bouquetin* (French) or *steinbock* (German). These squat, sturdy animals live and graze in herds; one noble buck with a harem of females. The male sports a pair of majestic, scimitar-shaped horns marked with a series of knobbles, like arthritic joints. These horns are used in battle as they fight for control over the herds, usually in the autumn rut.

On the scenic belvedere from Cabane du Mont Fort to Col Termin, known as the Sentier des Chamois (Stage 6), ibex are likely to be seen at close quarters. A large herd lives nearby on a hillside designated as a wildlife sanctuary. Another herd may be seen near Cabane de Prafleuri.

RECOMMENDED MAPS

MAPS OF THE Swiss survey, *Landeskarte der Schweiz* (L.S. or *Carte nationale de la Suisse*), are among the finest in the world. By artistic

The Aiguille du Drus on the early stage of the walk to Argentière (Stage 1)

Mont Blanc, seen from the path to Col de Balme (Stage 2)

The Glacier du Trient, from the path to Refuge les Grands (Alt. Stage 2)

Stage 3 ends at the lakeside village of Champex

The Ried glacier from Gasenried (Stage 12a)

use of shading, contours and colouring, the line of ridges and rock faces, the flow of glaciers and streams, the curve of an amphitheatre, narrow cut of a glen, the expanse of a lake and forest cover of a hillside all announce themselves clearly. A picture of the country immediately leaps from the paper.

At the head of each stage of the walk a note is given with regard to the specific map recommended for that particular stretch. In each case I have chosen the 1:50,000 series as this should be perfectly adequate for most needs. The greater detail provided by the 1:25,000 series is not likely to be required on this route, given the amount of waymarking on the ground. (No less than 9 sheets would be needed of 1:25,000 scale.)

Standard coverage at 1:50,000 scale runs into five sheets (numbers 282T, 283T, 273T, 274T and 284T), but we are fortunate in that the L.S. has published a double-sheet coverage for this particular area, so only two sheets are actually needed. These are:

    5003 Mont Blanc – Grand Combin
    5006 Matterhorn – Mischabel.

Please note that the most recent printing (1999) of 5006 does not show the route of the Europaweg from Gasenried to Zermatt, nor the position of the Europa Hut. However, the five standard-sized sheets have major paths usefully overprinted in red, and the 1999 edition of number 284T does indicate the route of the Europaweg – but not the location of the Europa Hut, which was only opened in the summer of 1999.

Addresses of map suppliers are given in Appendix C.

USING THE GUIDE

A BRIEF WORD of explanation about this guidebook. Distances are given throughout in kilometres and metres. Heights quoted are in metric too. These details are taken directly from the map, but in attempting to measure the actual distance of each day's walk I have made the nearest estimation I could. (With countless zig-zags it is impossible to be precise.) Likewise, **times are approximate only and make no allowance for rest stops or photographic interruptions** – for these you will need to add at least another 25% to the day's total. Inevitably these times will be found slow by some walkers, fast by others. By comparing your times with those given here (or quoted on signposts along the route) you will soon discover how much our pace differs, and adjustments can then be made when calculating your own progress through the day.

The Combin massif dominates the view from the Sentier des Chamois (Stage 6)

Throughout the text route directions 'left' and 'right' apply to the direction of travel, whether in ascent, descent or traverse. However, when used in reference to the banks of glaciers or streams, 'left' and 'right' indicate the direction of flow, ie: looking downwards. Where doubts might occur a compass direction is also given.

I have attempted to avoid an over-use of abbreviations in the guide, but it is inevitable that some have been adopted. All should be easily understood, but the following list is given for clarification:

C–Z	Chamonix to Zermatt, the Walker's Haute Route
hrs	hours
km	kilometres
L.S.	Landeskarte der Schweiz (maps)
m	metres
mins	minutes
PTT	Post Office (Post, Telephone & Telegraph)
SAC	Swiss Alpine Club
TGV	Trains à Grande Vitesse (the French superfast train)
TMB	Tour of Mont Blanc

Finally, I have made every effort to check the route as described for accuracy, and it is to the best of my belief that the guidebook goes to press with all details correct. However, changes do occur from time to time with paths re-routed and certain landmarks altered. Any corrections required to keep the book up-to-date will be made in future printings where possible. Should you discover any changes that are necessary (or can recommend additions with regard to accommodation, places of refreshment, etc) I would very much appreciate a brief note to that effect. A postcard sent to me via the publisher would be gratefully received.

STAGE 1:

CHAMONIX – ARGENTIÈRE

Distance:	**9 kilometres**
Time:	**2 hours**
Start altitude:	**1037m**
High point:	**Argentière 1251m**
Height gain:	**214m**
Map:	**L.S. 5003 Mont Blanc–Grand Combin 1:50,000 or L.S. 282T Martigny 1:50,000**
Accommodation:	**Chamonix – hotels, youth hostel, camping**
	Les Praz de Chamonix (35 mins) – hotels, camping
	Argentière – hotels, gîte
Transport options:	**Train & bus (Chamonix–Argentière)**

This initial, very short stage is suggested as a prelude for walkers who arrive in Chamonix late in the day and wish to get a few kilometres under their boots before seeking overnight accommodation. Those who arrive early and fresh enough from their travels can, of course, combine this with Stage 2 and continue over Col de Balme to Trient for an eight-hour day.

It's a valley walk without any passes to tackle. But it's a pleasant valley walk all the same, with one or two short ascents to contend with. It begins by threading a way among the crowds that throng the streets of Chamonix and heads upvalley on the road leading out of town, but then takes a path through woods and across open glades with a wonderful introductory view of the Drus standing guard over the Mer de Glace. Crossing the Arveyron the walk enters Les Praz de Chamonix, then over the river Arve onto another woodland path that is followed most of the way to Argentière.

Chamonix's valley is dominated by the Mont Blanc massif whose jagged aiguilles form fenceposts of granite and whose glaciers hang in

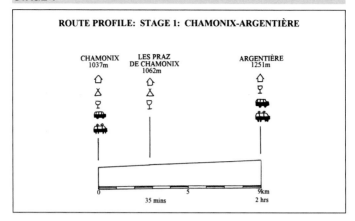

ROUTE PROFILE: STAGE 1: CHAMONIX-ARGENTIÈRE

sheets of arctic splendour above the town and its neighbouring forests. On the walk to Argentière there are several opportunities to gaze upon such scenes, while the bare northern wall with the russet-coloured Aiguilles Rouges is largely hidden from view.

As early as 1741 Chamonix – then a small village – was 'discovered' by Richard Pococke and William Windham, whose Account of the Glaciers or Ice Alps in Savoy *sowed the seeds of popularity for the valley; a popularity that has steadily increased from a lowly trickle to the present-day deluge of tourists who threaten an overkill with almost a million visitors per year in Chamonix alone.*

Footpaths along the valley are busy during the summer, and will remain so for the first three stages; that is, until the route of the Tour of Mont Blanc (TMB) has been left behind. During the high season there's likely to be a heavy demand for accommodation.

CHAMONIX[1] (1037m) *Hotels, youth hostel, camping, restaurants, shops, banks, PTT, tourist information, railway, buses, cableways and funicular.*

From Chamonix railway station walk down the main street, Avenue Michel Croz,[2] alongside shops and restaurants, and take the first road breaking to the right. This is Rue Whymper,[3] with a small garden on the corner. Continue straight ahead along the road signposted to Les Praz and Argentière, and soon leave the town behind.

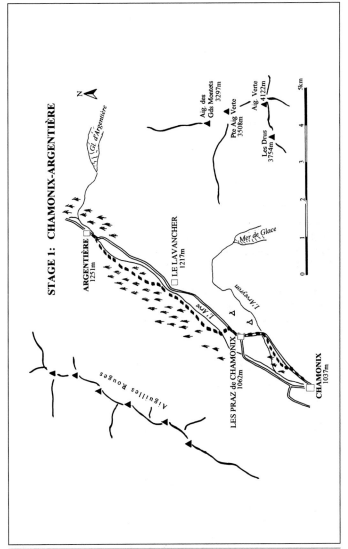

STAGE 1: CHAMONIX-ARGENTIÈRE

Shortly after passing the Chamonix–Mont Blanc road sign (15 mins from the station) note a bus stop on the left, and a sign on the right to La Frasse and Les Coverays. Immediately after the bus stop turn left over a bridge, then take the right-hand of two paths. This leads through the Bois du Bouchet. On coming to a crossing track turn right and soon gain a very fine view of the spear-like Drus ahead. At a crossing road continue ahead, and when the path veers right to enter a tunnel, leave it in favour of a minor path which takes you onto the road where it crosses the Arveyron (30 mins). Turn left and walk into **LES PRAZ DE CHAMONIX** (1062m 35mins *hotels, camping, restaurants*).

When you reach a roundabout cross directly ahead beside a small church in the direction of Argentière and Martigny. Immediately after passing the Hotel Les Rhododendrons the road curves to the right where you gain another splendid view of the Drus. Take the first turning left and wander past the Hotel Le Labrador. When the service road ends continue ahead on a gravel track alongside the river Arve. About 45 minutes after leaving Chamonix station the track crosses the river. Ignore the initial path on the right, but stay on the track which curves right just beyond and is signed Bois du Paradis. The track becomes a narrow metalled lane. When it forks continue ahead and shortly come to the café/bar Le Paradis des Praz (*refreshments*). Beyond this the way continues as a pleasant forest walk beside a stream.

Ignore all bridges that tempt across to the right-hand side of the Arve, and at path junctions follow signs for Argentière. About 1 hour 5 mins from the start a choice of routes is given. One crosses the river and is signed to Argentière via Les Tines, the other remains on the left of the river and is signed Argentière par Riviére Droite d'Arve. This is our path. It briefly hugs the river bank, then climbs steeply among trees above the railway (a fine restrospective view shows the Chamonix aiguilles). At a path junction continue ahead.

From here to Argentière the way is straightforward, remaining left of the river until at last you come onto the main road near Hotel Les Randonneurs. Wander up the road into **ARGENTIÈRE**,[4] passing the 3-star Hotel Montana, and about 100m beyond come to the *gîte d'étape*, Le Belvedere, about 2 hours from Chamonix railway station.

ARGENTIÈRE (1251m *hotels, gîte d'étape [Le Belvedere] 52 dortoir places, meals provided:* ☎ *(04) 50 54 02 59 restaurants, shops, PTT, tourist information, railway and bus links with Chamonix, cableways, etc*).

Note: In case of difficulty finding accommodation here, try Les Moulins des Frasserands (*dortoir – breakfasts available, but no evening meals*) about 2 kilometres upvalley.

Places or Features of Interest Along the Way

1: CHAMONIX: With the close proximity of Mont Blanc, Chamonix has always been at the forefront of alpine mountaineering, and during the development of alpinism in the 19th century it became a serious rival to Zermatt. Today it is unquestionably the leading mountaineering centre of Europe, if not the world. But the town's importance extends beyond the limits of mountaineering, for in winter it is a major ski resort, while in summer Chamonix attracts a veritable deluge of general tourists. It has plenty to occupy them, including the cable-car to the summit of the Aiguille du Midi, and from there the possibility of traversing the whole range by cableway to Entrèves, near Courmayeur in Italy. The railway to Montenvers has long been one of the most popular excursions, with its climax being superb views along the Mer de Glace to the Grandes Jorasses. The Chamonix valley, of course, offers excellent walking opportunities. (See *Chamonix–Mont Blanc – a Walking Guide* by Martin Collins [Cicerone Press]). Although the classic Tour du Mont Blanc does not actually visit Chamonix itself, it does traverse the valley. (See *The Tour of Mont Blanc* by Andrew Harper [Cicerone Press].)

2: MICHEL CROZ: The Haute Route begins by wandering down Avenue Michel Croz, named after one of the finest guides of the Golden Age of Mountaineering, a man whose talent and skills were discovered by Alfred Wills and then put to good use by Edward Whymper. Croz was a Chamonix guide (born in Le Tour in 1830) whose list of first ascents includes the Barre des Écrins, Mont Dolent, Aiguille d'Argentière, Dent Blanche, Grandes Jorasses and the crossing of the Moming Pass above Zinal. In 1865 Croz was in Whymper's party that made the first ascent of the Matterhorn, but was tragically killed on the descent. (See *Scrambles Amongst the Alps* by Edward Whymper.)

3: EDWARD WHYMPER: On leaving Avenue Michel Croz the route turns into Rue Whymper. Whymper will forever be remembered as the man who first climbed the Matterhorn, and as such is known far beyond the somewhat limited circle of active mountaineers. Whymper was a

London-born wood engraver who first visited the Alps in 1860 in order to make a series of sketches for the publisher William Longman. The following year he began a remarkable climbing career (often with Michel Croz) that included first ascents of the Écrins, aiguilles of Trélatête and Argentière, Grand Cornier, Grandes Jorasses (west summit), Aiguille Verte and, of course, the Matterhorn. He did little climbing in the Alps after the Matterhorn tragedy, but explored farther afield – making journeys to Greenland, the Andes of South America and three trips to the Canadian Rockies. His *Scrambles Amongst the Alps* is still considered to be one of the finest of all mountaineering books, and is frequently republished. Whymper died in Chamonix at the age of 71.

4: ARGENTIÈRE: A compact village at the upper end of the Chamonix valley. The original village stands on the true left bank of the Arve below the terminal moraine of the Argentière Glacier, an attractive huddle of chalets and a small church. Argentière makes a low-key alternative to Chamonix for a mountaineering or skiing base. The 'new' village which has grown astride the main valley road has a range of accommodation, plenty of restaurants and food stores and a tourist information office.

STAGE 2:

ARGENTIÈRE – COL DE BALME – TRIENT

Distance:	12 kilometres
Time:	5–5½ hours
Start altitude:	1251m
High point:	Col de Balme 2204m
Height gain:	953m
Height loss:	925m
Map:	L.S. 5003 Mont Blanc–Grand Combin 1:50,000 or L.S. 282T Martigny 1:50,000
Accommodation:	Le Tour (1 hour 30 mins) – hotel, gîte
	Col de Balme (3 hours) – refuge
	Le Peuty (5 hours 15 mins) – gîte, camping
	Trient – dortoirs
Transport options:	Bus (Argentière–Le Tour)
	Gondola lift (Le Tour–Charamillon–Les Grandes Otanes near Col de Balme)
Alternative route:	Col de Balme–Col de la Forclaz via Refuge Les Grands-Dessus – see Alternative Stage 2

For a first full day's walking this is a convenient and relatively undemanding stage. There's plenty of height to gain and lose, but the crossing of Col de Balme is not at all severe and walkers fresh from the U.K. have an opportunity to get into their stride with ease. Views on the way to the pass, when you look back through the length of the Chamonix valley, are dominated by Mont Blanc and its aiguilles, while the col itself gives a magnificent vision of the Monarch of the Alps shining its great snow dome and sending long glacial tentacles into the valley.

The Swiss frontier runs through Col de Balme, so all the descent

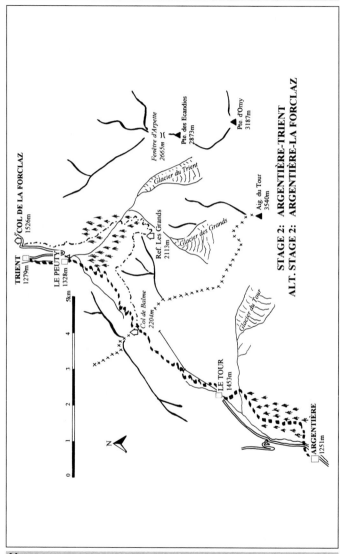

STAGE 2: ARGENTIÈRE-TRIENT
ALT. STAGE 2: ARGENTIÈRE-LA FORCLAZ

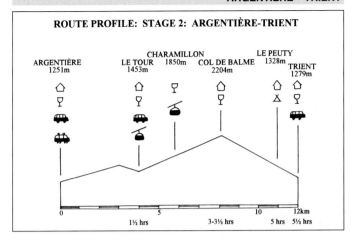

ROUTE PROFILE: STAGE 2: ARGENTIÈRE-TRIENT

(and the rest of the walk to Zermatt) will be within Swiss territory. Vistas of Mont Blanc are shunted into memory, although in days to come sudden surprise views will draw the eye back to the west and that great crown of snow.

The valley of Trient into which you descend is green and pastoral. There are no major peaks nearby, of either snow or rock, to match the grandeur of France behind you, but the scene from the col is not short of beauty, for to the north a line of mountains indicates the crest of the Bernese Alps, with Les Diablerets, Wildhorn and Wildstrubel just discernible.

Much of this stage is shared with the route of the TMB so you will no doubt meet plenty of other walkers during the day.

From the centre of Argentière take the road heading to the right (east), passing the PTT and Office du Tourisme and crossing the river (l'Arve) with the Glacier d'Argentière[1] seen hanging from its great shelf directly ahead. At a junction of streets bear right into the Chemin de la Moraine, and you will come to the line of the Mont Blanc Express railway. Pass beneath this and onto a track going ahead towards woods where you join the Petit Balcon Nord. A few metres after passing a chalet bear left. The way is signed to Le Tour and Le Planet.

Rising steadily among trees you will come to a path junction (**LES

AUGES 1412m 30 mins) where you continue straight ahead. Emerging from the woods the path narrows and gradually loses height with the village of Le Tour seen below, and Col de Balme directly ahead. Cross a stream draining the Glacier du Tour and walk on into **LE TOUR** (1453m 1–1½ hours *Accommodation: Chalet Alpin du Tour [CAF gîte]* ☎ *(04) 50 54 04 16, Hotel l'Olympique; restaurant, water supply, public toilets, telephone, bus to Chamonix, gondola lift).* Walk to the roadhead by the gondola lift.

Note: If you prefer to take the easy way to Col de Balme, ride the gondola lift to its upper station at Les Grandes Otanes, from which a short contouring path leads to the col.

The main path to Col de Balme passes along the right-hand side of the gondola lift station, and continues ahead on a broad track/ski piste. Before long a waymarked footpath breaks away to the right (it is signposted) where you enjoy views to Mont Blanc. This climbs easily up to the middle station of the gondola lift (**CHARAMILLON** 1850m *refreshments*). Just above it a path forks right away from ours on the way to the popular Albert Premier refuge below the Aiguille du Tour, passing the Gîte d'Alpage (*refreshments*). Ignore this option and maintain direction, gaining height without undue effort to reach the **CHALET-REFUGE COL DE BALME** (2204m 3–3½ hours *accommodation, refreshments*). The refuge has 26 places ☎ (04) 50 54 02 33, it stands on the unmarked Franco/Swiss border and purchases can be made in either French or Swiss francs.

The col makes a wonderful viewpoint. To the south stands the snowy mass of Mont Blanc[2] and its guardian aiguilles – Aiguille Verte and Drus being predominant in that view, while the Aiguilles Rouges line the right-hand wall of the valley.

Groups of ebullient walkers occupied all the seats outside the refuge, and most of those inside too. To a man they were all tackling the TMB and enjoying the cameraderie such a sociable walk inspires, greeting each new arrival with rude remarks having established an easy rapport during the days in which they'd shared the same paths, valleys and passes. They were heading south on the closing stages of their classic walk, while we were going in the opposite direction, against the tide, as it were. I looked back at Mont Blanc, then ahead to a grid of distant ridges that both teased and enticed. Col de Balme held the key to a wonderland.

Le Tour – the highest village in the Chamonix valley

Veer left beyond the refuge to a signpost at a footpath junction, then go right to begin the descent. (Trient is 2 hours from the col.) The path goes down in long loops at first, but once you enter forest the way steepens with tighter zig-zags. It brings you into a rough pastureland where you bear left to cross the Nant Noir stream and walk down to **LE PEUTY** (1328m 5–5¼ hours *gîte accommodation at Refuge du Peuty* ☎ *(079) 217 12 62, camping nearby*).

Continue down the road for a further 10 mins to the village of **TRIENT**.[3]

TRIENT (1279m 5–5½ hours) *Dortoir accommodation at Relais du Mont Blanc* ☎ *(027) 722 46 23 and Le Café Moret* ☎ *(027) 722 27 07; food store, PTT, Postbus link with Martigny. Office du Tourisme, 1921 Trient* ☎ *(027) 722 19 29.*

Note: In case of difficulty finding accommodation here, try Hotel du Col de la Forclaz 3 kilometres uphill to the east. Bedrooms and *dortoir* ☎ *(027) 722 26 88.*

Places or Features of Interest Along the Way

1: GLACIER D'ARGENTIÈRE: This major icefield flows from the great basin formed by the curving ridges of the Tour Noir, Mont Dolent, Aiguille de Triolet, Les Courtes and Les Droites. Mont Dolent is the lynchpin of this system, and on its summit the frontiers of France, Italy and Switzerland meet.

2: MONT BLANC: As the highest mountain in Western Europe Mont Blanc (4807m) has been the focus of mountaineering attention for more than two centuries. In 1760 wealthy Geneva scientist Horace-Bénédict de Saussure (1740–99) offered a prize for the first man to reach its summit. Several attempts were made in the ensuing years, but it was not until 8 August 1786 that Michel-Gabriel Páccard, the Chamonix doctor, and Jacques Balmat, a crystal hunter, reached the top. (Saussure himself made the third ascent in 1787.) Tourist ascents followed, then attention was focused on neighbouring aiguilles and new routes to already claimed summits. Among the outstanding developments mention should be made of the Brenva Ridge in 1865, Peuterey Ridge (1927), Route Major (1928), Gervasutti Pillar (1951) and Central Pillar of Freney in 1961. But whilst practically every face, pillar, ridge and couloir has been explored, Mont Blanc still retains its charisma, and to non-mountaineers no less, its undisputed grace and beauty. (For a history of the mountain, see *Savage Snows* by Walt Unsworth [Hodder & Stoughton, 1986].)

3: TRIENT: A small village set in a narrowing of the valley of the same name below La Forclaz. In spite of its being the first Swiss community met on this walk, it is nevertheless very French in both architecture and atmosphere. It is in an ideal situation to tackle the crossing of both the Fenêtre d'Arpette and Col de la Forclaz for the next stage of the route to Champex.

ARGENTIÈRE – COL DE BALME – LES GRANDS – COL DE LA FORCLAZ

Distance:	**15 kilometres**
Time:	**6½–7 hours**
Start altitude:	**1251m**
High point:	**Col de Balme 2204m**
Height gain:	**953m**
Height loss:	**676m**
Map:	**L.S. 5003 Mont Blanc–Grand Combin 1:50,000 or L.S. 282T Martigny 1:50,000**
Accommodation:	**Col de Balme (3 hours) – refuge**
	Les Grands (4½ hours) – refuge
	Col de la Forclaz – hotel, *dortoir*
Transport options:	**Bus (Argentière–Le Tour)**
	Gondola lift (Le Tour–Charamillon–Les Grandes Otanes near Col de Balme)
Alternative route:	**Col de Balme–Trient direct – see Stage 2**

This alternative stage is a very scenic one, giving close views of glaciers and distant views of crowding mountains and hinted valleys. The first section as far as Col de Balme is the same as that used by the main Stage 2, but thereafter the ways diverge with this alternative taking a *variante* of the TMB which passes a small refuge that does not always have a guardian in residence, so should you plan to stay there it would be wise to carry food. A steep descent below Refuge Les Grands brings you to a bridge over the torrent draining the Glacier du Trient, followed by a lovely path alongside a *bisse* (an irrigation channel) to the hotel on Col de la Forclaz. A splendid day's walk.

Follow directions to Col de Balme as set out in Stage 2 above. This will

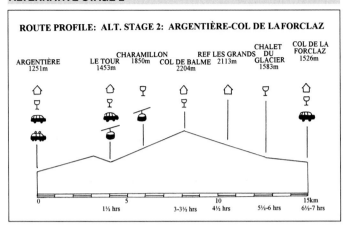

ROUTE PROFILE: ALT. STAGE 2: ARGENTIÈRE-COL DE LA FORCLAZ

take 3–3½ hours. A few paces before reaching the Chalet-Refuge bear slightly right at a footpath junction signed to Les Grands, Chalet du Glacier and Col de la Forclaz. The path contours for about 5 minutes, then descends a little along the right-hand hillside; in places the trail is narrow, but clear throughout. Having descended a short way it resumes a hillside traverse with views down to Trient and Col de la Forclaz.

About 40 minutes from Col de Balme, and having crossed a rocky section, the path turns a spur to gain a view into the upper reaches of the Trient valley and across to the Fenêtre d'Arpette. Now the hillside is clothed with bilberry and alpenrose, and as the way advances so the path climbs again with the Glacier du Trient seen ahead, and the smaller Glacier des Grands above to the right – superb alpine scenery. Topping a high point at about 2150m the Refuge Les Grands can be seen below. The path descends directly to it.

REFUGE LES GRANDS-DESSUS (2113m 4½ hours *15 places, cooking facilities, water supply; guardian sometimes in residence; owned by SAC – reservations* ☎ *(026) 658 13 23*)

The path descends directly below the hut, quite steeply in places, and soon slants across a rock face with fixed cable for safety. It then resumes in steep zig-zags, passes a couple of small ruins and enters pinewoods.

On coming to a fork in the path ignore the right-hand option (which leads to Alpage des Petoudes) and continue ahead, eventually reaching another path junction by a footbridge spanning a glacial torrent. (If you plan to stay in Trient bear left here – the village is about 50 minutes down-valley.)

Cross the bridge to another path junction. A few paces to the right **CHALET DU GLACIER** 1583m offers *refreshments*; the path which continues beyond it leads to the Fenêtre d'Arpette. We however turn left alongside the *Bisse du Trient* on a charming near-level path to reach **COL DE LA FORCLAZ**[1] **(**1526m *accommodation, refreshments, shop*) in another 50 minutes.

HOTEL DU COL DE LA FORCLAZ (1526m 6½–7 hours *Bedrooms and dortoirs*, ☎ (027) 723 18 07 E-mail: *forclaz@rooms.ch*

Places or Features of Interest Along the Way:

1: COL DE LA FORCLAZ: The path from Chalet du Glacier to the col was originally laid with rails in order to transport ice from the Trient glacier to the hotel on the pass. As for the road which crosses Col de la Forclaz, thereby linking Martigny with Chamonix, this was built between 1825–1887. The first motor vehicles crossed in 1912, with a maximum approved speed of 18 km per hour – none were allowed to make the journey by night. In 1864 Edward Whymper came across the Forclaz and was constantly bothered by what he called 'parasitic children' who pestered him and other travellers on the road. "These children swarm there like maggots in a rotten cheese," he wrote. "They carry baskets of fruit with which to plague the weary tourist. They flit around him like flies; they thrust the fruit in his face; they pester him with their pertinacity. Beware of them! – touch not their fruit... It is to no purpose to be angry; it is like flapping wasps – they only buzz more."

Distance:	14 kilometres
Time:	6½–7 hours
Start altitude:	1279m
High point:	Fenêtre d'Arpette 2665m
Height gain:	1386m
Height loss:	1199m
Map:	L.S. 5003 Mont Blanc–Grand Combin 1:50,000
	or L.S. 282T Martigny 1:50,000
Accommodation:	Arpette (6 hours) – hotel/*dortoir*, camping
	Champex – hotels, pensions, dortoirs, camping
Transport options:	Postbus (Trient–Col de la Forclaz–Martigny)
	Train (Martigny–Orsières)
	Bus (Orsières–Champex)
Alternative route:	Col de la Forclaz/Alp Bovine in place of Fenêtre d'Arpette – see Alternative Stage 3

The crossing of Fenêtre d'Arpette is a classic outing and one of the most demanding of the whole walk. The approach to it is full of interest with the frozen cascades of the Glacier du Trient's icefall in view nearly all the way, while the descent into the lovely pastoral Val d'Arpette begins with a wild and untamed wilderness of scree and boulders, but finishes with joyful streams, spacious woods and meadows. These contrasts are bound to bring pleasure to all Haute Route trekkers, for it is in such contrasts that long distance mountain routes gain much of their appeal.

The path is a good one practically all the way, but care should be

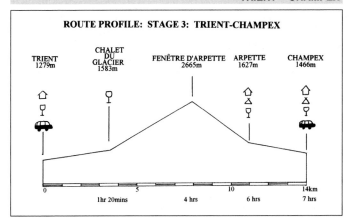

ROUTE PROFILE: STAGE 3: TRIENT-CHAMPEX

exercised on the initial descent from the pass where boulder fields are crossed. A twisted ankle here could have serious consequences.

At the end of the day Champex is the first 'real' Swiss village of the route, with attractive chalets facing the sun and boxes of flowers at the windows. It's a popular, welcoming little resort that has grown along the shores of a small reedy lake, and is noted for its magnificent alpine garden – considered by many to be the finest in Switzerland.

Note: *An alternative approach to Champex, which is less demanding than the Arpette crossing, yet still a very pleasant walk in its own right, is the so-called 'Bovine' route also adopted by the Tour of Mont Blanc. In suspect weather it would be preferable to the crossing of Fenêtre d'Arpette, and is detailed as Alternative Stage 3 below.*

Above the church in Trient walk up the main Col de la Forclaz road to a sign on the left which directs the way to the Sentier du Bisse-Glacier along a broad grass track which rises in long easy loops. At a junction of tracks continue ahead to regain the road. Cross directly ahead onto the continuing track which soon narrows to a footpath, zig-zags again and comes to a lovely *bisse* path where you turn right. (A *bisse* is an irrigation watercourse.) Follow this path all the way to the **CHALET DU GLACIER** (1583m 1hour 20mins *refreshments*).

Note: Walkers who spent the night at the Hotel du Col de la Forclaz and plan to use the Fenêtre d'Arpette route should cross the road in

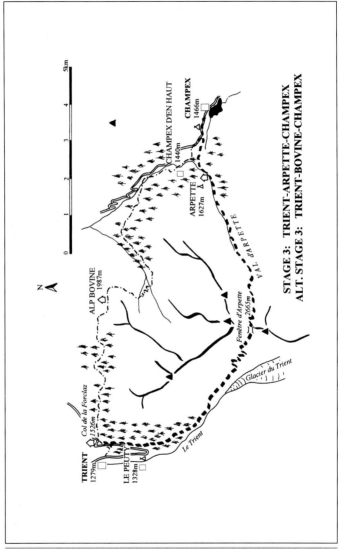

STAGE 3: TRIENT-ARPETTE-CHAMPEX
ALT. STAGE 3: TRIENT-BOVINE-CHAMPEX

front of the hotel where a signpost directs the path as Bisse du Trient – 50 minutes to the Chalet du Glacier.

The path forks at the Chalet du Glacier. Bear left and climb uphill to another fork. Once more take the left branch (the right-hand, lower, path goes to the glacier) where the climb to the pass begins in earnest, first among woods, then above these on a more open stretch with clear uninterrupted views onto the glacier. As you gain height so the Aiguilles Dorées and Pointe d'Orny grow above you to the south.

The gradient steepens, but the path is always clearly defined, even when crossing rocky slopes. Few paths allow such detailed study of an icefield in all its tortured glory as this does, and views are consistently magnificent. But the pass remains a well-kept secret until you're almost there.

A last scramble over a jumble of rocks brings you finally to the **FENÊTRE D'ARPETTE** (2665m 4 hours). This wild and rocky cleft makes a splendid pass, for the ridge it breaches is very much a division; to the west all mountains and glaciers owe allegiance to Mont Blanc, while to the east lies a new world – a stony world rather than an arctic one, and it will be three more days before you again feel the brush of glacial air on your face. The three-day intermission goes from bare rocks to pasture and forest through a neat and tended landscape, a brief respite before the high mountains are regained. The Fenêtre d'Arpette is a geological hyphen, and from it you gaze eagerly to the east and south-east where an array of ridges jostle the horizon and the Combin massif gleams a splash of white against the sky – a promise of good things to come.

We reached the pass in time to eat our lunch, emerging from a cool wind to bright sunshine and sun-warmed rocks on the Arpette side. But the walking world had come to the Fenêtre too, for everywhere we looked tanned bodies were spread across the rocks like basking seals. Not for nothing is this pass known locally as the Champs d'Elysses. Thank the popularity of the Tour of Mont Blanc[1] for that, for the pass is on a much-loved TMB Variante. Ten thousand people a year walk that circuit. How was I to know they would all be gathered that very day on the Fenêtre d'Arpette?

At first the descent drops into a rough, stony bowl at the head of Val d'Arpette. Caution is advised for the initial 100 metres or so where each one of an assortment of paths is particularly steep and, at times,

On the way to the Fenêtre d'Arpette the path climbs above the Trient glacier

loose under foot. Below this you cross a chaotic boulder field before the path (waymarked over the boulders) treats you with more respect and eases into Val d'Arpette proper.

Pastures and fruiting shrubs are a welcome relief after the barren rocks of the upper valley, and in almost two hours from the pass you come to a group of farms where a track leads onto the right bank of the stream. Five minutes later you reach the **RELAIS D'ARPETTE** (1627m 6 hours *accommodation [beds & dortoir], camping, refreshments* ☎ *(027) 783 12 21).*

Just beyond the hotel turn off the main track/road and take a footpath on the left that descends among trees and follows a stream. On coming to a bridge cross over, then go right on a footpath waymarked with green stripes. Recross the stream and soon after bear left when the path forks.

The fast-running brook you now accompany is a leat, or *bisse* – a watercourse created to direct part of a stream into a new valley, or to bring water to otherwise dry farmland. The Valais region has many such watercourses. One was followed at the start of the day, and there will be several more to follow in the days ahead. The path eventually brings you out of the woods at a small pond by a chairlift station. Go onto the road and bear right into **CHAMPEX**.[2]

CHAMPEX (1466m 7 hours) *Accommodation (hotels, pensions, dortoirs, camping), restaurants, shops, banks, PTT, bus link with*

Orsières and Martigny. Office du Tourisme, 1938 Champex-Lac ☎ (027) 783 12 27

Lower-priced accommodation: Pension En Plein Air (dortoirs & beds) ☎ (027) 783 23 50 – E-mail: hotelgite-en-plein-air@yahoo.fr; Au Club Alpin (dortoir) ☎ (027) 783 11 61; Au Rendez-vous (b&b) ☎ (027) 783 16 40; Auberge de la Foret ☎ (027) 783 12 78.

Arriving in Champex late in the afternoon we sought dortoir accommodation and were soon booked in, with surprisingly up-market comfortable beds in a dormitory with curtains dividing the room to allow a degree of privacy not normally experienced in such places. I went for a shower and came out at the same time as a Dutchman whom we'd met the previous evening in Trient. We both had wet towels and socks to dry so went onto the balcony outside our room to hang them out overnight. As we stood there, suddenly the balcony floor gave way beneath us and crashed onto the pavement, leaving the Dutchman and me hanging from the rail high above the street. We were wondering how to swing back into our room in safety when a shout from below caught our attention. It was a German trekker who'd also been in Trient the previous night. "This looks good," he called, waving his camera. "Hold it there, I would like a photo of this."

Places or Features of Interest Along the Way:

1: TOUR OF MONT BLANC: This classic, scenically spectacular walk makes a circuit of the Mont Blanc massif by way of the seven valleys that surround it. The TMB has numerous *Variantes*, but the standard route is some 190 kilometres long and takes about 10 days to complete. With some justification it is one of the most popular long-distance routes in Europe. See *The Tour of Mont Blanc* by Andrew Harper (Cicerone Press).

2: CHAMPEX: Also known as Champex-Lac to emphasise its lakeside position, this modest-sized village has developed as an all-year resort. During the summer there's swimming in a heated pool, boating and fishing in the lake. The alpine garden (*Jardin Alpin Florealpe*) above the village on the hillside to the north contains more than 4000 plants, and is generally reckoned to be the finest collection in Switzerland.

ALTERNATIVE STAGE 3:

TRIENT – COL DE LA FORCLAZ – ALP BOVINE – CHAMPEX

Distance:	16 kilometres
Time:	5½ hours
Start altitude:	1279m
High point:	Alp Bovine 1987m
Height gain:	876m
Height loss:	657m
Map:	L.S. 5003 Mont Blanc–Grand Combin 1:50,000
	L.S. 282T Martigny 1:50,000
Accommodation:	Col de la Forclaz (45 mins) – hotel, *dortoir*
	Alp Bovine (2½ hours) – emergency *dortoir* only
	Champex d'en Haut (4½ hours) – auberge/gîte, hotel
	Champex – hotels, pensions, *dortoirs*, camping
Transport options:	Postbus (Trient–Col de la Forclaz–Martigny)
	Train (Martigny–Orsières)
	Bus (Orsières–Champex)
Alternative route:	Trient–Fenêtre d'Arpette–Champex – see Stage 3

This route is the bad-weather alternative to the more demanding Fenêtre d'Arpette crossing, but it should not be assumed that it is an uninteresting walk. Far from it. It's a green and pleasant way, among forest and pasture and with good views down into the Rhône valley and across to the Bernese Alps that rise on the northern side. Since this is the path of the main TMB (the Fenêtre route is a Variante*) it is well-used, but the vast majority of walkers will be coming towards you.*

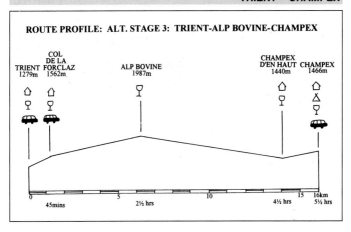

ROUTE PROFILE: ALT. STAGE 3: TRIENT-ALP BOVINE-CHAMPEX

From the church in Trient walk up to the main Col de la Forclaz road and bear right along it. Look for a sign on the left to Sentier du Bisse-Glacier, a broad grass track which swings up the hillside in easy loops. At junctions follow signs for Col de la Forclaz (this soon leaves the *bisse* route), and eventually the track brings you onto the road where a path runs along the left-hand side. After several hundred metres a sign directs you across the road and up a grass slope to **COL DE LA FORCLAZ** (1562m 45 mins *accommodation – Hotel du Col de la Forclaz; beds and dortoir* ☎ *(027) 722 26 88 – refreshments, shop*).

Immediately over the col on the east side a sign for the Bovine route points the way along the edge of a meadow beside a cattle byre, and progresses on the top edge of a sloping pasture before twisting in and out of woodland and gaining height with views into the Rhône valley. Working a way round the Combe des Faces, in about 1½ hours come to a junction of paths (1725m) where you continue ahead, still rising in forest.

After about 1 hour 45 minutes the way passes to the left of a group of alp buildings (**LA GIÈTE** 1884m) in an open grass basin, beyond which the path resumes in larch- and pinewoods. Shortly after a short contouring section that gives direct views onto Martigny, the trail rises to a high point on the edge of woodland from which the buildings of Alp Bovine can be seen a short distance ahead. The way now eases down to reach the alp 10 minutes later.

ALP BOVINE (1987m 2½ hours *refreshments, emergency accommodation only*) sits in a gentle slope of pasture with views north-east along the Rhône valley. The continuing path contours for a few minutes heading east, then curves south along the hillside before crossing a minor stream and descending steeply into more woodland. (The L.S. map is in error here, failing to show the true extent of this woodland.)

The rough sloping pastures of La Jure (with excellent bilberries in late summer) are crossed about 50 minutes beyond Alp Bovine, then you descend an open slope to a track which eases round the hillside and brings you to the farm buildings of **PLAN L'EAU** (1330m 3 hours 50 mins *refreshments*) which has a small buvette. From here the track becomes a narrow metalled road, but 2 minutes beyond the farm you break off to the right on a signed path which rises to woodland.

When the path forks in the forest take the left branch. Soon pass below a group of chalets and come to a road at **CHAMPEX D'EN BAS** (1299m 4 hours 10 mins). Turn right, pass the strung-out houses of this little village and at the upper end continue straight ahead at a minor crossroads.

In 4½ hours come to **CHAMPEX D'EN HAUT** (1440m *accommodation*) where you pass alongside the Chalet Bon Abri, an auberge/gîte with *dortoir* accommodation – open all year ☎ (027) 783 14 23. Just beyond this there's the large Hotel-Club Sunways ☎ (027) 783 11 22. After another 300m join the main valley road and turn right, rising to a high point at 1498m, then sloping downhill with the snow-crowned Grand Combin seen ahead, and come to **CHAMPEX**.

CHAMPEX (1466m 5½ hours) *Accommodation (hotels, pensions, dortoirs, camping), restaurants, shops, banks, PTT, bus links with Orsière and Martigny. Office du Tourisme, 1936 Champex-Lac ☎ (027) 783 12 27.*

Lower-priced accommodation: Pension En Plein Air (dortoirs & beds) ☎ (027) 783 23 50 – E-mail: hotelgite-en-plein-air@yahoo.fr; Au Club Alpin (dortoir) ☎ (027) 783 11 61; Au Rendez-vous (b&b) ☎ (027) 783 16 40; Auberge de la Foret ☎ (027) 783 12 78.

STAGE 4:

CHAMPEX – SEMBRANCHER – LE CHÂBLE

Distance:	**13 kilometres**
Time:	**3½–4 hours**
Start altitude:	**1466m**
Low point:	**Sembrancher 717m**
Height loss:	**749m**
Height gain:	**104m**
Map:	**L.S. 5003 Mont Blanc–Grand Combin 1:50,000 or L.S. 282T Martigny 1:50,000**
Accommodation:	**Sembrancher (2 hours 45 mins) – hotels, camping**
	Le Châble – hotels, pension
Transport options:	**Bus (Champex–Orsières)**
	Train (Orsières–Sembrancher–Le Châble)

Leaving Champex the route departs from that of the Tour of Mont Blanc and footpaths will be less busy. On this stage a gentle downhill walk followed by a pleasant valley stroll makes a good cushion between two rather strenuous days. Although there are no passes to cross, and no big glacier-hung mountains close at hand, it is by no means a dull day, for the path takes you into an everyday working Switzerland. A Switzerland that rarely appears in tourist brochures, but which nevertheless is good to see. There are small farming communities along the way, patches of hillside being cultivated far from chocolate-box resorts, and all with a general air of pastoral well-being.

If you were so inclined, Le Châble could be reached in a stiff morning's walk. But there's little to gain by rushing, for the onward route to Cabane du Mont Fort is too far to be achieved on top of this stage. Take the opportunity to enjoy a leisurely amble down to Sembrancher, and from there stroll into Val de Bagnes and make the most of your time.

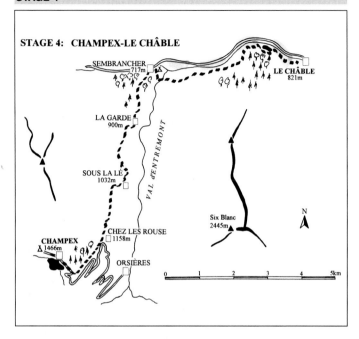

STAGE 4:   CHAMPEX-LE CHÂBLE

Wander through Champex village heading south-east alongside the lake, and at the far end where the road forks at Hotel Grand Combin, take the left-hand branch. Rounding a dog-leg bend you come to the end of the road at Hotel Alpina. Ahead are two footpaths. Take the right-hand one descending into woods; signposted to Orsières it loses height with a steady gradient. On coming to cross-tracks continue ahead. This will bring you to a track near the Champex–Orsières road.

Do not go round to the road but cross directly ahead onto a continuing path sloping downhill. This joins a more easily angled track leading to the head of a dirt road (at least it was a dirt road in the summer of 2000; it may now be metalled). Maintain direction to a continuing track.

At a junction of tracks near the hamlet of **CHEZ LES REUSE** (1158m), do not descend to the hamlet but continue straight ahead,

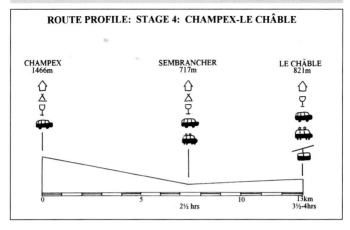

ROUTE PROFILE: STAGE 4: CHAMPEX-LE CHÂBLE

CHAMPEX
1466m

SEMBRANCHER
717m

LE CHÂBLE
821m

2½ hrs

3½-4hrs

joining another track coming from the right and soon cutting into a cleft above a small gorge. When it forks take the lower, right-hand branch which goes round pastureland, and you will come to another fork where this time you take the left-hand option. Before long come to a T-junction of trails; bear left and 15 metres later slant away to the right on a grass track signposted to Sous la Lé, La Garde and Sembrancher. The trail is waymarked and it brings you down to a gravel farm road above the small village of **SOUS LA LÉ** (marked as Soulalex, 1032m on the map).

Walk down to the village, and then head left at a water trough to go along a narrow street that leads to a junction of roads where you continue straight ahead, but instead of descending to a group of houses, take the left-hand track signposted to La Garde (25 minutes from here). Keep to the main, upper track when a choice is given, until a second track junction is reached immediately after crossing a partially hidden stream. Ignore that which cuts off left and continue ahead, now easing downhill among pastures to a junction of four tracks (**TETOU**). Go straight ahead on a path descending among trees and soon arrive in the village of **LA GARDE** (900m 1 hour 15 mins).

In the village pass a chapel on your right and walk along a street in the direction of St-Jean and Sembrancher, then down to a crosstracks (**LE CREUX**) where you go straight ahead, soon reaching a hairpin bend in a road. Once more continue ahead on a track again signposted to

St-Jean and Sembrancher, following power lines. Between here and Sembrancher there are various footpath alternatives, with directions indicated at all route junctions. Perhaps the most direct trail is that which passes to the left of the little chapel of St-Jean and descends through woodland, goes beneath a railway line and brings you into the centre of Sembrancher, a village sitting at the junction of Val d'Entremont and Val de Bagnes.[1]

SEMBRANCHER (717m 2½–2½ hours *accommodation, camping, refreshments, shops, bank, PTT, Postbus and railway*) is a stone-walled village with an attractive little square, which makes a good base for a walking holiday since it has access to two appealing valleys, and frequent public transport facilities.

Leave the village by walking upvalley on the road heading into Val d'Entremont, signposted (rather perversely) to Champex and Ferret. After 200 metres head left on a side road marked to Chamoille. Passing houses cross the river (la Dranse d'Entremont) and go straight ahead where the road forks at **LES MOULINS** (729m). The narrow tarmac road goes between low-lying pastures and fields with encouraging views ahead. When you come to a fork near a wooden cross take the left branch ahead. At another fork near a small fenced building, take the right branch on what is now a track, and wander up into forest.

Having gained height in the forest the track forks. Take the lower option, signed to Le Châble, and soon after break off on a waymarked footpath descending to the left. At the foot of the slope come onto a track at a hairpin bend. Go round this hairpin to the left and onto another track – the Promenade de la Dranse. Wander ahead alongside the Dranse de Bagnes, eventually coming to a narrow metalled road near a bridge. Do not cross the river but follow the road between meadows to enter **LE CHÂBLE**.[2]

LE CHÂBLE (821m 3½–4 hours) *Accommodation, restaurants, shops, banks, PTT, Postbus & cableway to Verbier, train to Martigny. Office du Tourisme, 1934 Le Châble* ☎ *(027) 736 16 82.*

Lower-priced accommodation: Pension Les Alpes Garni ☎ *(027) 776 14 65; Hotel La Poste* ☎ *(027) 776 11 69; Hotel du Gietroz (across the river in Villette)* ☎ *(027) 776 11 84.*

Places or Features of Interest Along the Way:

1: VAL DE BAGNES: Rising in an attractive cirque of mountains

Sunset view from Cabane du Mont Fort (Stage 5)

View of the Grand Combin with Lac de Louvie below (Alt. Stage 6)

Emerging from the ladders at Pas de Chèvres to a new landscape (Stage 7)

*The village square at
Sembrancher*

rimmed by the Swiss–Italian border south-east of the Grand Combin, the Val de Bagnes contains a diverse set of landscapes: from open tarn-flecked pastures to deep gorge-like defiles, and from bleak screes and seemingly barren moraines to forests and meadows full of flowers. There are several remote mountain huts, challenging trails and a number of walkers' passes, all of which make this a splendid base for a walking holiday – see *The Valais, a Walking Guide* by Kev Reynolds (Cicerone Press). Despite the fact that the valley is sparsely populated with only a few hamlets and even fewer villages, the Val de Bagnes commune is Switzerland's largest, and at 295 kilometres square is greater in extent than the cantons of Geneva, Schaffhausen and Zug.

2: LE CHÂBLE: Huddled on the left (west) bank of the Dranse de Bagnes, Le Châble is the valley capital, while its neighbour just across the bridge on the east side of the river is the more modern 'suburb' of Villette. Le Châble's village square has a very French appearance, but some of the old stone-walled farmhouses in the back streets pronounce their Valaisian authenticity by displaying over their doorways the horns of long-deceased cattle that have taken part in cowfighting, a purely local (Valaisian) tradition. Cable-car access with Verbier starts just across the river next to the railway station – Le Châble is the valley terminus of a branch line of the St Bernard Express which begins in Martigny. From the village a twice-daily Postbus service runs upvalley (July–Sept only) as far as the huge Mauvoisin dam, from where walkers and climbers set out on a 4 hour trek to the Chanrion hut.

STAGE 5:

LE CHÂBLE – CLAMBIN – CABANE DU MONT FORT

Distance:	9 kilometres
Time:	6–6½ hours
Start altitude:	821m
High point:	Cabane du Mont Fort 2457m
Height gain:	1636m
Maps:	L.S. 5003 Mont Blanc–Grand Combin 1:50,000 or L.S. 282T Martigny & 283T Arolla 1:50,000
Accommodation:	Le Cotterg (10 mins) – b&b
	Cabane du Mont Fort – SAC refuge
Transport options:	Postbus (Le Châble–Verbier)
	Cableway (Verbier–Les Ruinette)
	Cableway (Le Châble–Verbier–Les Ruinettes)

A first glance at the map gives little indication that a walking route can be made between Val de Bagnes and Cabane du Mont Fort without either extensive use of the steeply twisting road to Verbier, or the lengthy zig-zag road from Lourtier through Sarreyer.

But there is a route, and a delightful one at that. It is a combination of narrow lanes, tracks and footpaths – often steeply climbing, but always interesting. There are some fine villages, an attractive chapel, long forest sections with welcome shade on a hot day, high pastures and some truly magnificent views. With so much height to gain it is advisable to make an early start, take your time and enjoy everything the ascent has to offer. But before setting out you should telephone ahead to the refuge to reserve bed-space for the night – the telephone number for Cabane du Mont Fort is given at the end of the route details.

This walk avoids Verbier altogether in an effort to remain as far from

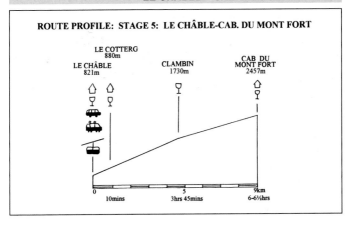

ROUTE PROFILE: STAGE 5: LE CHÂBLE-CAB. DU MONT FORT

LE COTTERG
880m
LE CHÂBLE
821m

CLAMBIN
1730m

CAB DU
MONT FORT
2457m

0
10mins

5
3hrs 45mins

9km
6-6½hrs

mechanisation as possible. It's impossible to escape all sign of the downhill ski industry, however, for Verbier and its surrounding hillsides offer a winter paradise for the skier, and an abundance of lifts and cableways have effectively laced the mountains like an old-fashioned corset. Whilst one deplores such desecration, thanks must be offered that a wholesale sacrifice has not been made to the transitory thrill of downhill skiing, that there are still ways for the wanderer to escape and that even here paths may be found that mostly ignore pylons, cables and bulldozed pistes.

It is on this stage that the Grand Combin begins to exert its influence. This great snowy massif dominates the Val de Bagnes (and, to an extent, Val d'Entremont too). It's the most westerly 4000 metre mountain of the Pennine Alps, an attractive, substantial block that cultivates a number of glaciers and whose presence is recognised for several days yet to come. Although the walk does not stray to it, the Combin nevertheless imposes its personality on the Haute Route trekker with its sheer size and grandeur. Since leaving Mont Blanc (whose bulk was always behind you) the Combin massif is the first on the walk to impress with such authority and grace.

From Le Châble cross the river to **VILLETTE** and bear left. (Initially the route is part of the Tour des Villages, and is waymarked with yellow diamonds or stripes outlined in black.) Head to the right past Café-

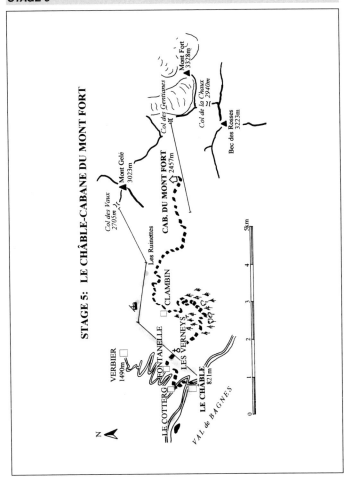

STAGE 5: LE CHÂBLE–CABANE DU MONT FORT

Restaurant La Ruinette and follow waymarks up through the village along narrow streets, passing houses and dark timber granaries, some of which are perched on staddle stones. In 10 minutes cross the Villette–Verbier road by Café Magnin and enter **LE COTTERG** (880m *b&b accommodation in La Chamade* ☎ *(027) 776 14 58)*. A signpost showing the way to Chapelle les Verneys (in 50 mins) directs the route to the right (ignore the sign to Cabane du Mont Fort, for this goes via Verbier). With waymarks and signposts as your guide a series of tracks and footpaths lead to **LA FONTANELLE**.

As you come to this hamlet, dug into the steep hillside, take a narrow footpath breaking away beside a wooden cross (dated 1982) to edge alongside an orchard (1045m 30 mins). An unmetalled road takes you round the hillside heading south-east, and eventually brings you to the small but elegant white chapel and few buildings of **LES VERNEYS** (1120m 1 hour *water supply, public toilet*).

Continue beyond the buildings for about 5 minutes, and when the track makes a right-hand hairpin, take a signed footpath leading uphill on the left. This goes into forest, gaining height steeply at times, in order to cross a scoop in the mountainside. This 'scoop' opens to a combe higher up. The way goes over a stream and climbs on, but having gained a high point you then descend a few metres to a junction of paths (1200m about 25 minutes from Les Verneys). Head to the left, rising once more in forest. The path is signposted to Verbier and Les Ruinettes, and waymarks are yellow and black.

This trail rises quite steeply on the right-hand (south) side of what soon becomes a distinctive combe and leads to a handful of timber buildings, above which you bear left on an unmetalled road, and when it forks soon after, take the upper track. This winds uphill in long loops with waymarked footpath short-cuts.

The footpath leads up to a pair of wooden buildings and passes between them (**LA COMBE** 1555m). A few paces beyond these the path forks (this may not be very clear). Take the lower option across the hillside combe, enter forest and continue for some way to a footpath junction at 1600m, where you bear right on a rising trail signed to Clambin and Les Ruinettes. (The path straight ahead at this junction goes to Verbier.) It's a steep ascent, but when you come out of forest to a small open patch of pasture, there's a wonderful view of the Combin[1] massif on the far side of Val de Bagnes. This is the first of many magnificent sightings, but the magic never fades.

Continue towards a stone-based chalet, but veer left before it and pass beside a timber chalet with Verbier[2] seen below in a large grassy basin. An easy path then brings you to a junction of tracks at **CLAMBIN** (1730m 3 hours 45 mins *refreshments*) – an attractive restaurant which enjoys a wonderful panorama is seen a short distance to the left. Go right, then immediately left on a track signposted to Les Ruinettes and Cabane du Mont Fort.

This track rises to another junction (**HATAY** 1844m) where you bear right and a few paces later slant left uphill and come to a picnic/barbecue area marked as **LE HATTEY** (1860m *water supply*). A broad ski piste has now been bulldozed down the hillside above Le Hattey, but the path crosses and recrosses this, climbing still in forest until emerging at last to spectacular views of the Grand Combin, and the Mont Blanc massif beyond intervening ridges in the south-west.

> *On this upward path we came upon an elderly Swiss couple descending. They wore smiles as bright as their red shirts and were so obviously enjoying their day out that we stopped to speak and shared with them a love of the morning, of the near views and far, and talked briefly of other mountains and valleys, of huts and villages, of glaciers and snowfields and birdsong and the fragrance of the forest – in general feeding off each other's enthusiasm. Then the lady whispered that her husband could now only walk up the gentlest of hills – but he'd swallowed his pride and taken the occasional chairlift or cable-car to enable him to reach the loftier viewpoints from which he was happy to walk down. "Well," she confided, "he is 82." With that my prejudices stacked against cableways in the mountains came crashing round me.*

On coming to a track by a cableway (5 hours 15 mins from Le Châble) turn right along it. Before long this rises as a path, and at a signed junction continues alongside a *bisse* to a dirt road. Cross this road to another narrow path which rises in a few paces to join another *bisse*. There are wonderful views still to Grand Combin and its neighbouring peaks and glaciers drawing you on. Follow the *bisse* path on an easy contour round the hillside leading to **CABANE DU MONT FORT**[3] which stands on a bluff at a junction of trails with exceptionally fine views.

CABANE DU MONT FORT (2457m 6–6½ hours) *80 places, meals and drinks available* ☎ *(027) 778 13 84.*

Places or Features of Interest Along the Way:

1: GRAND COMBIN: This large and impressive mountain has several

Clambin, on the ascent to Cabane du Mont Fort

distinct summits over 4000 metres. Standing entirely in Switzerland the summit crown has a splay of ridges from which busy glacial systems pour down; the largest being the great Glacier de Corbassière which falls in a series of terraces to the north, and is the largest icefield in the Western Pennine Alps. (A fine close view of these icy terraces is to be had from Cabane de Pannoissière, reached by a 4 hour walk from Fionnay.) Although several ascents were made of a secondary peak (Aiguille du Croissant) in 1857–58, the actual summit of Grand Combin (Combin de Graffeneire 4314m) was first climbed on 30 July 1859 by Charles St-Claire Deville, with the guides Daniel, Emmanuel and Gaspard Balleys and Basile Dorsaz. Nowadays the massif attracts ski mountaineers as well as summer-season climbers, and is frequently traversed by those tackling the winter Haute Route on ski.

2: VERBIER: One of the best-known ski resorts in the Alps, Verbier sprawls within a large natural basin of hillside high above the valley, a real sun-trap and an obvious site for development as a ski village since the amphitheatre that cradles it holds plenty of snow and the slopes are ideal for skiers of all standards. It has an over-abundance of mechanical lifts – 80 or so, if you include those in the neighbouring Val de Nendaz which is easily accessible from it. Thanks to the great ski boom of the 1960s, the original village of Verbier has been swamped by a rash of chalets, hotels and unattractive apartment blocks, but many footpaths lead from it to take the eager walker into scenes of peace and tranquility. (For information contact: Office du Tourisme, 1936 Verbier ☎ (027) 775 38 88; website: www.verbier.ch)

3: CABANE DU MONT FORT: Owned by the Jaman Section of the Swiss Alpine Club, this hut is superbly placed on a grassy bluff due south of Mont Gelé. Because of easy access by cableway, it is very busy by day when it is used as a refreshment stop by parties of walkers. It is also used extensively by ski-tourers in the spring. There are several high passes within easy reach, including Col de Chassoure, Col du Mont Gelé, Col des Gentianes, Col de la Chaux and Col Termin which are all crossed by walkers in summer. Unfortunately a lacing of cable-ways has devalued some of these passes, but others happily remain free from mechanisation. Views from the hut are splendid, with Grand Combin and the Mont Blanc massif taking pride of place, but the Dents du Midi are also on show. Sunsets are magnificent.

STAGE 6:

CABANE DU MONT FORT – COL TERMIN – COL DE LOUVIE – COL DE PRAFLEURI – CABANE DE PRAFLEURI

Distance:	14 kilometres
Time:	6–6½ hours
Start altitude:	2457m
High point:	Col de Prafleuri 2965m
Height gain:	885m
Height loss:	740m
Map:	L.S. 5003 Mont Blanc–Grand Combin 1:50,000 or L.S. 283T Arolla 1:50,000
Accommodation:	Cabane de Prafleuri – mountain refuge
Transport options:	None
Alternative route:	Col de la Chaux instead of Col Termin – see Alternative Stage 6

Before the present trek was established mountain walkers attempting to work out a traverse of the high country between Val de Bagnes and Val des Dix often sought ways to avoid the Grand Désert glacier draped down the northern flanks of Rosablanche. Alternative passes were tried, and long circuitous routes taken via the lower reaches of Val de Nendaz. But as the Grand Désert shrank back, so its crossing became fairly straightforward. For several years there were no major crevasses to worry about, and unroped walkers could tackle the ice without concern.

Then the glacier changed and a potentially dangerous crevasse opened up which made this crossing impractical for most walkers. Latest research shows a continuing speedy withdrawal of this glacier, which makes a diversion below the ice more appropriate as a safer option. The present route therefore drops below the glacier snout to a

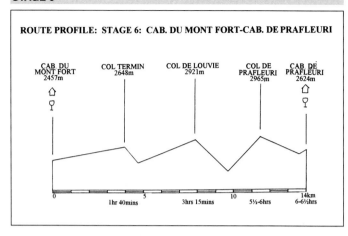

ROUTE PROFILE: STAGE 6: CAB. DU MONT FORT-CAB. DE PRAFLEURI

small lake, followed by an uphill slanting walk over rocks and screes to regain the original route. It's quite possible that in a few years' time the Grand Désert glacier will have shrunk back to such an extent that walkers will be able to traverse glacial slabs without need to descend to the lake. Until then, follow directions given below, but watch waymarks as a guide to the current situation.

The stage is full of variety and ever-changing views. At first there are vast panoramas, but as you wander along the high belvedere trail to Col Termin, so the Combin massif dominates the scene, and if you walk quietly and remain alert, you stand a good chance of seeing ibex on or near the path. (This is a noted wildlife sanctuary.) Later, on the eastern side of Col de Louvie, you are faced with a bewildering landscape of dying glaciers, chaotic moraines and large regions of seemingly barren wilderness. But even in such landscapes the majesty of the mountains impresses itself; yet one grows convinced (if you ever needed convincing) that the 'everlasting hills' are everlasting only in the words of the poet. On this walk you are witness to the ceaseless toil of erosion. The mountains are dying, falling apart, and to wander through their scenes of destruction is a sobering experience.

Under normal summer conditions the walk should present no major route-finding difficulties, but in poor visibility, or under threat of storm, problems may arise on the stretch between Col de Louvie (2921m)

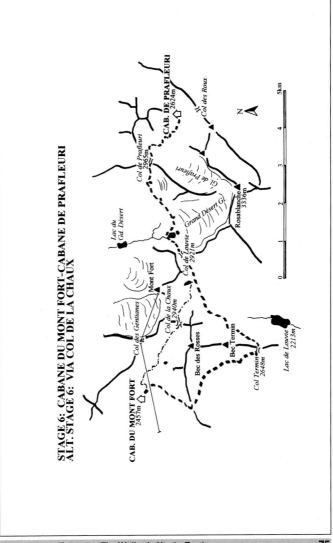

STAGE 6: CABANE DU MONT FORT–CABANE DE PRAFLEURI
ALT. STAGE 6: VIA COL DE LA CHAUX

and Col de Prafleuri (2965m) where there is no real path other than a trail of cairns and paint flashes. The Sentier des Chamois between Cabane du Mont Fort and Col Termin is also one to avoid under certain bad-weather conditions. Seek the advice of the guardian at Mont Fort in case of uncertainty. He may advise crossing Col de la Chaux as a safer option – this is described as Alternative Stage 6 below.

Note: *The following route is a long and tiring stage – remember that the time quoted (6–6½ hours) does **not** include rests of any kind, so it could take between 8–9 hours to get from one hut to the next. Fill your water bottle before setting out, and make sure you have food to sustain you on what could be the toughest day of the walk so far.*

Descend north-east from Cabane du Mont Fort to the major path junction where you head to the right on a path signed 'Tour du Val de Bagnes et Combin'. After a few metres the path forks. Bear left ahead and shortly come down onto a track which you descend to the second hairpin bend. Leave the track here in favour of a footpath which makes a traverse of the scree slope seen ahead. This is the start of the Sentier des Chamois. Beyond the screes the trail climbs at a steady gradient with beautiful views to enjoy. It becomes a fine belvedere of a path on which you may well catch sight of ibex (*bouquetin* in French).

In a little over an hour from the hut you reach a path junction where a trail breaks off to descend. Ignore this and continue straight ahead to cross another scree slope, climb over a spur (fixed chains to safeguard the way in icy conditions), and continue round the mountainside on a narrow but easy path that nevertheless has some exposed sections. Views remain magnificent; Grand Combin aloof across the valley, and the Val de Bagnes itself a very long way beneath the trail. Views back to the north-west show the Dents du Midi in the distance.

We were finding the path difficult to negotiate. Not that there were obstacles in the way, nor were conditions at all bad. Neither were we bothered by the steep slopes plunging to Val de Bagnes fifteen hundred metres below. Our problems arose from lack of concentration, for the glories of the Combin massif across the valley were so outstanding that our attention was being held by them – away from the first principle of safety on the path. It was difficult to take our eyes off that gleaming mass that had conjured a streamer of cloud just below the summit and was teasing as in a dance of the seven veils. The summit was clear, so were the lower slopes. But the midriff of the mountain was veiled. It was a tantalising view. Then, when we did correct our attention to review the way ahead, it was to spy a herd of twenty or so ibex moving unconcerned in morning shadow below us. They were very close, and completely unbothered by our presence.

Grand Combin from the Sentier des Chamois

The way then reaches the obvious saddle of **COL TERMIN** (2648m 1 hour 40 mins) in a shoulder of the Bec Termin which rises to the north. From here a very wild landscape rises to north and east, with Mont Fort and Rosablanche[1] both casting out high ridges to confuse.

Descend on the east side for a few metres, then veer sharply left on the path signposted to Col de Louvie and Prafleuri. (Steeply below lies Lac de Louvie – there's a refuge just beyond its southern end with one of the finest views in the Swiss Alps – worth remembering for a return visit to Val de Bagnes.) Fifteen minutes from the col another path breaks away and descends to the lake, but you ignore this and continue towards a wild-looking rocky cirque at the head of the Louvie valley. A rough boulder tip is crossed, but after this the path improves. Views remain impressive.

An hour from Col Termin come to a path junction where the left-hand option breaks away to Col de la Chaux and Mont Fort. Continue straight ahead, over a second boulder field and, skirting the left-hand side of a narrow stony valley (good waymarks and a clear path), you climb to gain the rocky **COL DE LOUVIE** (2921m 3 hours 15 mins).

A barren landscape greets you in the north-east; a wilderness of screes, moraine and the dying glacier spilling from Rosablanche. The Grand Désert is well-named.

Descending from the col the way hugs the left-hand side of a narrow, rocky little valley – again, well waymarked, although care is needed in places where there is no real path. As you lose height note a large red–white waymark painted on a boulder on the eastern side of the valley ahead, beyond the Grand Désert glacier – this is a guide for later. Follow the immediate line of waymarks and occasional cairns that lead down to the outflow stream at the northern end of a glacial tarn (2760m 3 hours 50 mins) below the snout of the Grand Désert. Over this turn right and make your way roughly south-east up and across a vast stony wasteland to a line of cairns and waymarks.

The route takes you past a number of little tarns and glacial ponds, crossing broad granite slabs and jumbled boulders. Waymarks are frequent, but in poor visibility it is absolutely essential not to lose sight of them. Take compass bearings where necessary.

Col de Prafleuri is seen at the head of what looks like a steep slope of scree. A small glacier flows down from Grand Mont Calme west of the pass, and the waymarked trail brings you to its edge where it is necessary to descend a short but steep and broken slope (sometimes snow or ice) in order to continue to the foot of the pass. Descend with care – a frustrating descent, for you have to climb again to reach the pass.

The climb to the col will no doubt be rather tiring as it involves working a way up a steepish slope of rough blocks and scattered rocks. So reach **COL DE PRAFLEURI** (2965m 5½–6 hours) to be greeted by a view south-east over a much-scarred and depressingly barren mountain bowl to Mont Blanc de Cheilon which dominates much of Stage 7.

Descend the steep path winding down to a level section beneath the Glacier de Prafleuri; cross levelled gravel beds to a track where you bear right, soon leaving this on a waymarked footpath that drops to the left into a grim-looking valley with a first sighting of **CABANE DE PRAFLEURI**.[2] The path takes you below the hut, so that the final approach is unfortunately up a steep path that deposits you at the hut doorway.

> **CABANE DE PRAFLEURI** (2624m 6–6½ hours) *59 places, manned April, and early July to end of Sept, meals provided.* ☎ *(027) 281 17 80 or (027) 207 30 67.*

Places or Features of Interest Along the Way:

1: ROSABLANCHE: This snow peak of 3336m offers easy ascent routes and a celebrated panorama from its summit – an exceptionally fine viewpoint from which to study larger peaks of the main Pennine chain. It is popular as a skiing expedition in spring, and from the Prafleuri hut by walkers in summer (2 hours from the hut by way of the Prafleuri glacier). It was first climbed in September 1865.

2: CABANE DE PRAFLEURI: Privately-owned, the original hut was constructed in the mid 1950s when quarrying work began below the Prafleuri glacier as part of the Grande Dixence hydro-electric scheme. (The hut was used to house site-workers in the early days.) Whilst it lacks any views of inspiration, it is particularly well-sited for walkers on the Chamonix–Zermatt route, for immediately above it to the south the easy Col des Roux gives access to Val des Dix. The old barracks hut was replaced in October 2000 by the present purpose-built hut. Ibex can often be spied nearby.

Distance:	**10 kilometres**
Time:	**5½ hours**
Start altitude:	**2457m**
High point:	**Col de Prafleuri 2965m**
Height gain:	**885m**
Height loss:	**740m**
Map:	**L.S. 5003 Mont Blanc–Grand Combin 1:50,000 or L.S. 283T Arolla 1:50,000**
Accommodation:	**Cabane de Prafleuri – mountain refuge**
Transport options:	**None**
Alternative route:	**Sentier des Chamois/Col Termin instead of Col de la Chaux – see Stage 6**

A more direct, and therefore slightly shorter route to Col de Louvie, the Col de la Chaux is seen behind Cabane du Mont Fort at the head of a stony hanging valley. Although it is rough under foot and without the wonderful views of the Sentier des Chamois–Col Termin main route described in the previous section, the Col de la Chaux crossing is preferable and safer under certain conditions. Should the guardian at Cabane du Mont Fort advise against using the Sentier des Chamois, this could be your best bet. Check locally for current conditions. During research rockfall had obliterated a large section of path leading to the col, but as it is a much-travelled route, one can expect the trail to have been reinstated by the time this guide goes into print. Comments at the head of the previous section with regard to the route from Col de Louvie to Col de Prafleuri are valid insofar as this Alternative Stage is concerned.

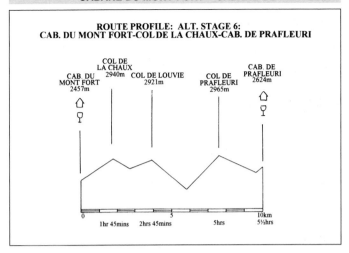

ROUTE PROFILE: ALT. STAGE 6:
CAB. DU MONT FORT-COL DE LA CHAUX-CAB. DE PRAFLEURI

Descend from Cabane du Mont Fort on an easy-angled track that winds into the stony basin to the east. As you enter the basin/hanging valley, note that there are two tracks pushing into it. Go to the upper track and follow this as it pushes upvalley, curving in long loops to gain height. After about 45 minutes come to a junction (2706m). The continuing track climbs to Col des Gentianes, but the Col de la Chaux path breaks away to the right. A few paces up this you pass a locked metal shelter.

The path, waymarked red–white, picks a way across a very stony terrain and passes above a small glacial lake. It then steers onto the left-hand slope of the hanging valley, guided still by waymarks and cairns where the path is thin or non-existent. Near the head of the valley a very large waymark painted on a rock below the col ensures you keep left of the shrinking Glacier de la Chaux.

So gain the rocky **COL DE LA CHAUX** (2940m 1 hour 45 mins) to exchange one desolate stony scene for another. Looking back you see beyond the coffee-coloured glacial tarn to Cabane du Mont Fort and the spiky Dents du Midi as a backdrop. Ahead lies another stony bowl, and across its bounding ridge the summit of Rosablanche can be seen with the Grand Désert glacier draped down its north-west face.

A steep descent path cuts left below the col, skirts the slopes of the basin then veers right (well waymarked) to cross a rocky shoulder from which the Grand Combin is once more on show. Here you find a junction of paths (2840m 2 hours 15 mins). That which descends ahead goes to Col Termin, while the left-hand path leads to Col de Louvie.

Take the Louvie path across ribs of rock and boulders, then descend to the right of a green glacial tarn to join another path where the letters T L and C are painted on a rock (T = Termin; L = Louvie; C = Chaux – the three col destinations). Take the left-hand option which rises as a good path to gain **COL DE LOUVIE** (2921m 2 hours 45 mins). Both the Mont Blanc massif and Grand Combin can be seen when looking back from here.

For the continuing route to Cabane de Prafleuri, please refer to Stage 6 above.

CABANE DE PRAFLEURI – COL DES ROUX – COL DE RIEDMATTEN – AROLLA

Distance:	**16 kilometres**
Time:	**6½ hours**
Start altitude:	**2624m**
High point:	**Col de Riedmatten 2919m**
Height gain:	**735m**
Height loss:	**1353m**
Map:	**L.S. 5003 Mont Blanc–Grand Combin 1:50,000 or L.S. 283T Arolla 1:50,000**
Accommodation:	**Refuge de la Gentiane la Barma (1 hour) – mountain refuge**
	Arolla – hotels, *dortoir*, camping
Transport options:	**Bus (Le Chargeur–Vex)**
	Postbus (Vex–Arolla)
Alternative route:	**Col des Roux–Cabane des Dix–Pas de Chevres instead of Col de Riedmatten – see Alternative Stages 7 & 7a**

The walk which leads from the rather gloomy, man-savaged Prafleuri glen to Arolla is a true delight. Given fine weather conditions the views on this stage will be among the very best of all. There's the surprise vision that greets you on arrival at the first col of the day (Col des Roux), for you emerge from morning shadow to the incredible sight of the Val des Dix spread before you – a five kilometre lake, green pastures and big mountains. Best of all of these mountains is the great pyramid-shaped Mont Blanc de Cheilon; but it has its handsome neighbours too, and as the day progresses so you draw closer to them, crossing Col de Riedmatten to descend beside Pigne d'Arolla, then below Mont Collon. Col de Riedmatten is in itself a revelation, a rocky cleft in the

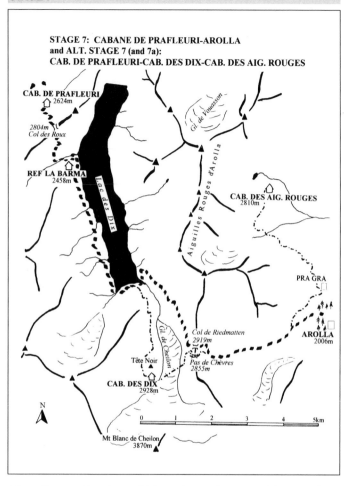

STAGE 7: CABANE DE PRAFLEURI-AROLLA
and ALT. STAGE 7 (and 7a):
CAB. DE PRAFLEURI-CAB. DES DIX-CAB. DES AIG. ROUGES

Monts Rouges ridge, from which you have a first view of the Matterhorn far off. (Make the most of it for you'll not see it again until you approach Zinal on Stage 10.)

Despite the fact that you have two passes to cross, this stage is not

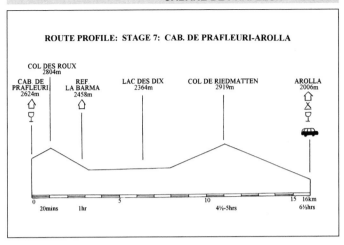

ROUTE PROFILE: STAGE 7: CAB. DE PRAFLEURI-AROLLA

unduly taxing, for by now you should be well into your stride and pacing the days in comfort. Only the last pull up to Col de Riedmatten is a little demanding, but once on the pass the beauty of the scene spread before you will put that momentary weariness into perspective.

Note: Alternative Stage 7 described below also makes a very fine day out with the opportunity to break the walk with an overnight spent in Cabane des Dix, which is dramatically situated beneath the great north face of Mont Blanc de Cheilon. Both routes on offer have much to commend them, but the Col de Riedmatten crossing is the more direct.

On leaving Cabane de Prafleuri walk upvalley for about 40 metres, then bear left (waymarking on rocks) to Col des Roux, an obvious pass just to the south of the hut and only 180 metres above it. The route is by way of a slope of boulders and rocks, but there's a good path which leads to it in easy zig-zags. In fact the ascent is achieved quickly and a lot more easily than might be imagined from below, and you come onto **COL DES ROUX** (2804m) in about 20 minutes, to be rewarded by a view almost guaranteed to stop you in your tracks.

Note: An alternative to the crossing of Col des Roux (in case of bad weather) is to go down-valley from the hut following the track on the right-hand side of the stream. This becomes a path which, rounding a rocky corner, overlooks the huge dam of Le Chargeur[1] at the northern end of Lac des Dix. The descent from hut to dam early in the season may be bothered by one or two snow chutes. If this is the case, take great care when crossing, for a slip could be serious. On reaching the dam bear right and follow the track along the west side of the lake. This goes through several tunnels, the first being the longest and darkest. A switch at the entrance gives five minutes of light, which is sufficient time to get through. Follow the track to the far end of the lake where you join the main route described.

The path forks on the saddle of Col des Roux. Go straight over to the south side and descend on a continuing trail that brings you to more boulders, but then becomes easier under foot. The path veers south-westward into the pastures of a shallow valley below the Glacier des Ecoulaies. Heading towards a lone farm (unnamed on the map, but marked as 2575m), you swing away to the left to cross a stream, then ease round the hillside and come to the stone-built **REFUGE DE LA GENTIANE LA BARMA**[2] (2458m 1 hour). This privately-owned refuge is permanently open, but not always manned. It has sleeping places for about 30, and cooking facilities. For enquiries and/or reservations contact: Café de Amis, Hérémence ☎ (027) 281 11 97. If you do use the facilities, please treat with respect and do nothing to abuse the hospitality offered.

Immediately before the refuge head to the left on a descending path to join the lakeside track where you bear right. The walk upvalley alongside Lac des Dix is a delightful one with little effort required. You can swing along with all senses alert to the wonders of the day, with marmots whistling from the trackside pastures, the clang of cowbells matching your stride. There are warning signs of rockfall, streams spilling down the hillsides, and snowgleam topping peaks ahead.

At the southern end of Lac des Dix come to a metal suspension bridge that crosses the south-eastern inlet. It's a slender bridge but a safe one, yet since you can see through the metal grid to the water below, it might give those who suffer vertigo an uneasy moment! On the far side a steel staircase leads to a small works building and a narrow path heads uphill from it.

This path initially takes you through a very flowery patch (edelweiss and field gentians) and then enters a stony valley carved by the Cheilon glacier. This valley grows wider as you head south, but on entering, it is narrow and littered with boulders. The path works a way along the left-hand side, over boulder fields and across streams, then

The Cabane des Dix (see Alternative Stage 7)

zig-zags to gain height. All the time Mont Blanc de Cheilon[3] gleams ahead, its glacier and long trough of moraine sweeping through the valley floor creating new landscapes for some future generation of Haute Route walkers to wander through.

> *Consider this: some far-off day pastures of lush grass will no doubt carpet this valley like so many further down. There'll be flowers in spring and early summer, cattle perhaps grazing where today only moraine grit and stone and dirty glacial ice spread their stark outlines. The mountains too will look somewhat different, and Mont Blanc de Cheilon will have lost its upper glaciers that at present drape its south, east and western flanks, and it may then take on a replica appearance of the Matterhorn, carved into a smooth-sided pinnacle by that very ice – as its north face has already been planed by the fast-receding glacier of Cheilon. Such is the destiny of these mountains and their valleys as erosion works its relentless toil.*

After a fairly lengthy level stretch the path suddenly swings left (eastward) and climbs to gain the narrow notch of **COL DE RIED-MATTEN** (2919m 4½–5 hours) and a window onto a new world.

Note: The final climb up the gully to the col can be aggravated by loose grit, and it requires some effort. An alternative is to break off to the right at the foot of the gully where waymarks take another path a short distance to the ladders of the Pas de Chèvres. There are three near-vertical ladders bolted to the rockface – *not* to be attempted by anyone suffering vertigo – at the top of which a path descends on the eastern side of the ridge to join that from Col de Riedmatten.

> *Trading shadows for sunshine on my first crossing of the col we gained that rocky cleft and light suddenly flooded ahead, washing a land of snow, ice, rock and a distant slope of grass. Below, the ridge fell into a basin of mountain-ejected debris, but our eyes were uninterested in any of this, for our attention was held by the crest of Pigne d'Arolla, by the great iced gateau of Mont Collon, by the sharp stiletto blade of the Matterhorn's upper reaches far off, by a vast wall of rock notable for the little spire of the Aiguille de la Tsa projecting from it, and by the snow-wrapped Dent Blanche on the far side of that wall.*

Note: For an even broader view than may be gained from the col, follow the narrow trail which bears left onto the ridge, but take care as it requires a little scrambling in places. It is only necessary to go a short distance to win a huge panorama.

Descending to the east the path is clearly defined although rather steep at first. It leads into an undulating grassy bowl where it then veers to the right and joins another path that comes down from Pas de Chèvres (crossed on Alternative Stage 7a). Now heading to the left (east) the path, clear and undemanding, takes you easily down towards Arolla. Mont Collon disappears from view, but Pigne d'Arolla[4] grows in stature on the right with the long Tsijiore Nouve glacier carving its way in a deep trench behind a grass-covered wall of moraine. Then, as you approach Arolla, so Mont Collon[5] reappears like an island in a sea of ice.

The path divides two or three times, but you simply follow the waymarked trail all the way down to **AROLLA**.[6]

AROLLA (2006m 6½ hours) *Accommodation (hotels, pension, dortoir), camping, restaurants, shops, PTT, Postbus link with Les*

Haudères and Evolène. Further information from: Office du Tourisme, 1986 Arolla ☎ (027) 283 10 83.

Lower-priced accommodation: Centre Alpin et la Jeunesse (dortoirs & rooms) ☎ (027) 283 19 09; Hotel Aiguille de la Tsa (dortoir – 15 mins below Arolla) ☎ (027) 283 14 06; Hotel du Glacier (also dortoir option) ☎ (027) 283 12 18; Hotel Mont Collon ☎ (027) 283 11 91; Hotel du Pigne d'Arolla ☎ (027) 283 11 65. Possible room(s) to rent – enquire at the village shop opposite the Post Office.

Places or Features of Interest Along the Way:

1: LE CHARGEUR: Constructed as part of the massive Grande Dixence hydro scheme that harnesses the waters of several Valaisian valleys, the huge dam known as the Barrage de la Grande Dixence which stands at the northern end of Lac des Dix is a stupendous piece of engineering, and at 284 metres is claimed to be the world's highest. From its base to the crest of the wall it stands twice as tall, with twice the volume, of the largest of Egypt's pyramids. It consists of 5,960,000 cubic metres of concrete and holds back some 400 million cubic metres of water.

2: REFUGE DE LA GENTIANE LA BARMA: Overlooking Lac des Dix this privately-owned refuge was originally part of a cheese dairy built in 1934 alongside cowsheds. The dairy was abandoned in 1964, then the buildings were acquired by the Gymnastic Society, La Gentiane, of Mâche (down-valley in Val d'Hérémence) who renovated them to create this delightful 30-place refuge.

3: MONT BLANC DE CHEILON: This shapely mountain, 3870 metres high, dominates the Val des Dix and towers over Cabane des Dix. Generally reckoned to be the finest peak in the Arolla district for rock and ice routes, it received its first ascent in September 1865 by the west-north-west flank which is reached from the Col de Cheilon. (This is the usual route today, and the one most often used in descent.)

4: PIGNE D'AROLLA: An easy snow mountain that neighbours Mont Blanc de Cheilon to the east, the Pigne is often ascended by ski mountaineers during a spring traverse of the classic Haute Route. An outstanding viewpoint, in one vast panorama most of the mountains of the Pennine Alps that feature in the Chamonix–Zermatt route can be seen, as too can the chain of the Bernese Alps. The Gran Paradiso and other peaks of the Graian Alps are also visible, and it has been claimed that the Mediterranean can be detected from the summit on a clear day. The first ascent was made by A W Moore, Horace Walker and their guide, the 'fearless' Jakob Anderegg, in July 1865. Its height is 3796 metres – a distinctive peak recognised from afar.

5: MONT COLLON: More than any other, Mont Collon is the dominant feature of the Arolla valley (the upper south-western arm of Val d'Hérens). Despite its modest altitude (3637m), the rocky buttresses, snow domes and apparent bulk give this mountain an imposing stature out of all proportion to its true size. Glaciers flow round its east and west flanks like icy calipers, effectively giving Mont Collon the appearance of an island peak, but to the south it is attached to the higher L'Evêque by way of the Col de la Mitre. Mont Collon was first climbed by G E Foster with H Baumann and J Kronig in 1867. There are several routes of varying grades adorning its face, pillars and ridges today.

6: AROLLA: This small mountaineering centre was one of the first to be 'adopted' by the British. In his book *The Alps*, R L G Irving says: "...at Arolla is the nearest thing to an imperial possession which England has in the Alps, an English church". In 1921 the skeletons of a man and a chamois, along with a rifle and coins dating from before 1850, were unearthed by a shrinking glacier. The village, which is attractively set among woods of larch and Arolla pine, is slowly expanding, but it remains one of the smallest of those on the Walker's Haute Route. As a base for a mountaineer's first alpine season it takes a lot of beating, while it also makes a very fine walking centre. (See *The Valais* – a walking guide also published by Cicerone Press, for ideas.)

ALTERNATIVE STAGE 7:

CABANE DE PRAFLEURI – COL DES ROUX – CABANE DES DIX

Distance:	11 kilometres
Time:	4–4½ hours
Start altitude:	2624m
High point:	Tête Noir 2981m
Height gain:	797m
Height loss:	440m
Map:	L.S. 5003 Mont Blanc–Grand Combin 1:50,000or L.S. 283T Arolla 1:50,000
Accommodation:	Refuge de la Gentiane la Barma (1 hour) – mountain refuge
	Cabane des Dix – SAC refuge
Transport options:	None
Alternative route:	Via Col de Riedmatten to Arolla – see Stage 7

This alternative to the main route described above has much to commend it. Although it is described only as far as the Dix refuge, it should be feasible for most Haute Route trekkers to continue as far as Arolla (another 2½–3 hours) by way of the Pas de Chèvres. Walkers choosing this option, however, should be aware that the onward route from Cabane des Dix involves crossing the Glacier de Cheilon to the Pas de Chèvres. This glacier has a route marked across it in most summers, is heavily used and should cause no disquiet as crevasses are virtually non-existent at the point of crossing.

The first part of the walk is the same as that taken on Stage 7, but departs from it at the southern end of Lac des Dix. From here a path leads along the left (west) bank moraine of the Cheilon glacier, climbs over a shoulder of the rock promontory called the Tête Noir and drops below the hut.

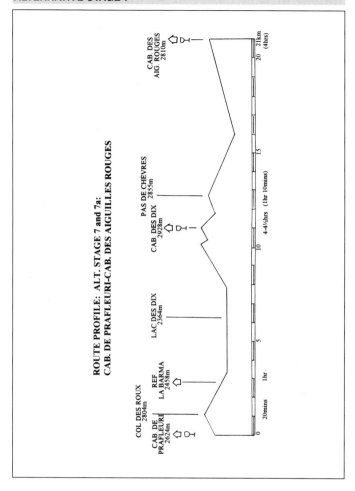

**ROUTE PROFILE: ALT. STAGE 7 and 7a:
CAB. DE PRAFLEURI–CAB. DES AIGUILLES ROUGES**

Cabane des Dix occupies a truly spectacular site with a direct view onto the north face of Mont Blanc de Cheilon. It is, however, an extremely busy hut and all intending to use it for overnight lodging are urged to telephone their reservation in advance.

Follow route directions as for Stage 7 as far as the southern end of Lac des Dix (2½ hours). About 50 metres before the suspension bridge at the end of the track, head off to the right on a path that climbs steeply and is signposted to Cabane des Dix.

At first the path rises over abrupt slopes of grass and rock, but eases as you gain the crest of a lateral moraine of the fast-receding Glacier de Cheilon. The path is clear and views ever-interesting, and as you make progress along the moraine, so you can see the deep col of Pas de Chèvres (the continuation route from the hut) on the far side of the glacier.

Towards the end of the moraine the path veers right, descends into the ablation valley, then rises over grass slopes and onto screes by which you gain the north-west shoulder of the Tête Noir which hides not only Mont Blanc de Cheilon, but also the Cabane des Dix.

As you rise towards the saddle on this shoulder, a wonderful panorama is seen off to the left (east). Far beyond the ridge of the Monts Rouges a jagged collection of peaks holds your attention. In that collection is the Matterhorn, whose profile from here is quite different to that normally seen from Zermatt. It appears as a distant stiletto with a marked shelf projecting to the south just beneath the summit. Then, when you gain the saddle, the vast pyramid of the north face of Mont Blanc de Cheilon appears before you, while below the hut can be seen perched on top of a rocky knoll. The path winds down into a glacial plain, crosses a stream or two, then strikes directly up the slope to reach the **CABANE DES DIX**.

CABANE DES DIX (2928m 4–4½ hours) *150 places, restaurant service, guardian in residence from mid-March to mid-May, and from July to mid-Sept ☎ (027) 281 15 23. Owned by the Monte Rosa section of the Swiss Alpine Club, this refuge is one of the busiest in the Alps and is patronised by walkers, climbers and ski-tourers alike.*

Note: For the continuing route to Arolla and/or Cabane des Aiguilles Rouges, see Alternative Stage 7a below.

CABANE DES DIX – PAS DE CHÈVRES – CABANE DES AIGUILLES ROUGES/AROLLA

Distance:	**10 kilometres (6 km to Arolla)**
Time:	**4 hours (2½–3 hours to Arolla)**
Start altitude:	**2928m**
High point:	**Cabane des Dix 2928m**
Height loss:	**540m (957m)**
Height gain:	**428m (30m)**
Map:	**L.S. 5003 Mont Blanc–Grand Combin 1:50,000 or L.S. 283T Arolla 1:50,000**
Accommodation:	**Cabane des Aiguilles Rouges – mountain refuge**
	Arolla – hotels, pension, dortoirs, camping
Transport options:	**None**
Alternative route:	**Via Lac des Dix and Col de Riedmatten to Arolla – see Stage 7**

The walk to Cabane des Aiguilles Rouges maintains the intrinsic character of the high route and the trekker opting for this gains by visiting one of the most attractive alps in Switzerland (Pra Gra), and also by enjoying spectacular views from the hut across the Arolla valley to its steep eastern wall. What is missing, of course, is a visit to Arolla itself.

Cabane des Aiguilles Rouges is situated in a somewhat barren rocky landscape immediately below the ridge after which it is named. The aiguilles are not seen at their best from the hut, however, due to foreshortening, but they may be viewed in all their glory on the way to Col de Torrent on Alternative Stage 9, and also from one or two passes further east.

As forewarned, this stage crosses the Cheilon glacier, on the far side of which there's the option of crossing either Col de Riedmatten (as per Stage 7) or the near-vertical ladders to Pas de Chèvres. The ladders are clearly seen before the path forks, so if the prospect of tackling these does not appeal, you'd better choose the Riedmatten alternative.

From Cabane des Dix descend the knoll on a clear path that winds leftwards (south) to the edge of the rubble-strewn Glacier de Cheilon, and then head north-east across it. Marker poles, cairns and waymarks give directions. It's an easy crossing with practically no crevasses, but it is important to follow the precise line shown by the markers.

On reaching the far side continuing waymarks and cairns steer you slanting left towards the base of Col de Riedmatten (crossed on Stage 7). The route takes you over a chaos of rocks and boulders, and can be quite tiring. On gaining a clear path coming from Lac des Dix and leading to Col de Riedmatten, bear right and a few paces later the path forks. The left-hand option climbs to Col de Riedmatten, while the right-hand path goes to the ladders of the Pas de Chèvres.

This latter path rises to hug the base of the ridge, and traverses beneath it as far as the foot of the ladders. There are now three, the middle one much longer than the others. Each one is near-vertical and securely attached to the rock face, but care should be exercised – especially when carrying a large rucksack. One or two rungs are so close to the rock face that only the toes of your boots can gain purchase, and at the top of the second ladder it is necessary to step to the right onto a flat rock before climbing the final one. (Some walkers may feel the need of a safety rope.)

So reach the **PAS DE CHÈVRES** (2855m 1 hour 10 mins) where a very fine panorama unfolds. This includes the Veisivi–Bertol wall above Arolla, with the delicate little Aiguille de la Tsa projecting from it, and beyond that the top of Dent Blanche, summit cone of the Matterhorn, Mont Collon and many more. It's a col to relax on and enjoy before tearing yourself away to tackle the descent.

An easy path takes you down on the eastern side, at first quite steeply, into a basin of rough grassland to join another path coming from the neighbouring Col de Riedmatten. The walk down towards Arolla follows a clear trail, much-trodden by walkers and climbers. On the right Pigne d'Arolla towers in a sweep of rock and ice, with the long Tsijiore Nouve glacier bulldozing a huge trough behind a grass-covered moraine wall. Views are consistently lovely. When you reach a broad track breaking away to the left, leave the Arolla path and head off along it.

Arolla-bound walkers: Simply continue down the path. It forks several times above the village, but all paths lead to Arolla unless otherwise signposted. The final approach is through pleasant woodland. (See Stage 7 for further information.)

The track winds round the hillside, then brings you to the cluster of alp huts of **PRA GRA** (2479m), an idyllic setting of grey stone-roofed chalets, barns and cattle-byres on a green terrace.

Continue ahead (north-westward) on a broad path across pastures and on to a wide plateau. The path now swings left into a region of boulder slopes and gravel beds with streams running through. Above this hang a small glacier and scoops of snow. Across the streams the way veers right to tackle more boulder slopes and scree, and on a short section a fixed chain gives reassurance when the path is icy. The final climb to the **CABANE DES AIGUILLES ROUGES**, set on a rib of rock and scree, becomes a little steep, but is none too arduous.

CABANE DES AIGUILLES ROUGES (2810m 4 hours) *80 places, meals and drinks available when the guardian is in residence (July to mid-Sept)* ☎ *(027) 283 16 49. It is owned by the Club Alpin Académique of Geneva.*

Note: For details of the continuing walk to Lac Bleu, where you rejoin the main route, see Stage 8.

The track which leads from La Gouille to Les Haudères (Stage 8)

Val de Zinal, from the path near Barneuza (Stage 11)

Zinalrothorn seen from the descent to Zinal (Stage 10)

Distance:	**10 kilometres**
Time:	**4 hours**
Start altitude:	**2006m**
Low point:	**Les Haudères 1452m**
Height loss:	**554m**
Height gain:	**215m**
Maps:	**L.S. 5003 Mont Blanc–Grand Combin and 5006 Matterhorn–Mischabel both 1:50,000 or L.S. 283T Arolla 1:50,000**
Accommodation:	**La Gouille (1 hour 45 mins) – pension**
	Les Haudères (3 hours) – hotels, pension, *dortoir*, camping
	La Sage – hotel, *dortoir*
	Villa (+ 15 mins) – simple rooms (self-catering only)
Transport options:	**Postbus (Arolla–Les Haudères–La Sage–Villa)**
Alternative route:	**Cabane des Aiguilles Rouges–Lac Bleu – see below**

Although this is a short and reasonably undemanding stage, it is not really practical to go beyond La Sage (or Villa) as neither the crossing of Col du Tsaté nor Col de Torrent offers prospects of accommodation for at least another five hours. It is nonetheless a stage to enjoy for there are numerous features to brighten the way.

The route to Les Haudères by way of Lac Bleu is designed to avoid all but the very briefest of sections of road walking, in addition to providing an excuse to visit one of the best-loved sites around Arolla. There are charming views when you gaze back the way you have

Evelene

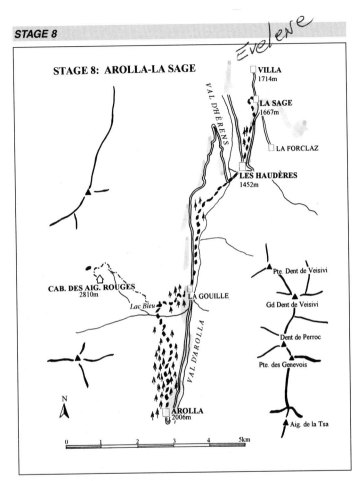

STAGE 8: AROLLA-LA SAGE

VILLA
1714m

VAL D'HÉRENS

LA SAGE
1667m

LA FORCLAZ

LES HAUDÈRES
1452m

CAB. DES AIG. ROUGES
2810m

Lac Bleu

LA GOUILLE

VAL D'AROLLA

Pte. Dent de Veisivi

Gd Dent de Veisivi

Dent de Perroc

Pte. des Genevois

N

AROLLA
2006m

Aig. de la Tsa

0   1   2   3   4   5km

come, there are woodlands and small meadows, and between Lac Bleu and La Gouille a small alp hamlet where you can buy fresh milk and cheese. From La Gouille a wooded path leads to some lovely old houses on the edge of Les Haudères, a mountaineering centre at the head of Val d'Hérens, where it forks into the tributary glens of Arolla and Ferpècle. Then, leaving Les Haudères a steady rising traverse path ascends the hillside to La Sage.

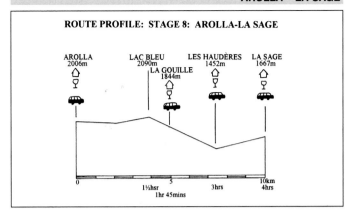

ROUTE PROFILE: STAGE 8: AROLLA-LA SAGE

Note: *Before setting out on this stage it is advisable to telephone ahead to book rooms for the night as there's limited accommodation in both La Sage and Villa. Failure to secure beds in either of these places will necessitate a return to Les Haudères. If this should happen it might be worth taking an early Postbus next morning to La Sage (for the Col du Tsaté route) or Villa (for the Col de Torrent option).*

From the village square by the Post Office in Arolla walk down the side road towards Hotel du Glacier. About 50 metres before the hotel bear left on a narrow footpath which climbs above some buildings, then bears right along the hillside to reach the Centre Alpin. Take the continuing footpath along the wooded hillside. Soon come to a junction of paths and bear right on an easy contour among larch and juniper. The path forks. Bear left and wind uphill and shortly come to another unmarked fork. Continue ahead (ignoring the left-hand option) along a comfortable gradient for a while before climbing again to yet another unmarked junction where you bear right. In 20 minutes cross a stream below an alp hamlet. Beyond this the trail continues a traverse of open hillside where it is worth pausing to enjoy views back to Mont Collon and Pigne d'Arolla.

The route develops into something of a switchback, an undulating trail that absorbs the natural line and takes you over two or three more streams, from the largest of which you overlook Satarma in the valley below, then up onto an open grassy bluff overlooking the aptly-named

LAC BLEU (2090m, 1½ hours). Once again there's a fine view back to Mont Collon, although Pigne d'Arolla has disappeared at this point.

Alternative Route (Cabane des Aiguilles Rouges to Lac Bleu)

Go above the hut a short way on a rising path heading north (direction arrows painted on rocks), then drop steeply, first towards the east to cross a stream, then south-eastward on a clear path. Descending steeply through different layers of vegetation the way brings you directly to **LAC BLEU** (1 hour).

Go down to the tarn's outflow and along a footpath to a tiny alp hamlet (**LOUCHE**) where cheese and milk may be purchased. Pass to the right of the hamlet and descend through forest to **LA GOUILLE** (1844m 1 hour 45 mins *accommodation, refreshments, Postbus to Les Haudères*), a small hamlet set beside the Arolla/Les Haudères road. Bear left down the road for about 200 metres, then slope off to the right on a path waymarked yellow and black. This eases along the hillside below the road and soon joins a track near a tiny white-painted chapel. Continue down the track, and when it forks wander straight ahead.

With gentle gradients the track leads down-valley and eventually comes to a group of handsome old timber houses. Just beyond these join the main road, bear right and walk into **LES HAUDÈRES**.[1]

LES HAUDÈRES (1452m 3 hours) *Hotels, dortoir, camping, restaurants, shops, PTT, Postbus. Office du Tourisme, 1984 Les Haudères* ☎ *(027) 283 10 15.*

Lower-priced hotels: Des Alpes ☎ *(027) 283 16 77; Edelweiss* ☎ *(027) 283 11 07; Gai-Logis (garni)* ☎ *(027) 283 14 13; Des Mélèzes* ☎ *(027) 283 11 55; Veisivi* ☎ *(027) 283 11 01; dortoir at Colonie Le Foret* ☎ *(027) 283 10 47.*

After crossing the bridge at the village entrance bear right on the road heading towards Ferpècle, La Forclaz and La Sage, but then turn left opposite Hotel des Alpes. Wander along a narrow street lined with attractive, typically Valaisian timber buildings, and follow through on an upper village street where there are both direction signs and waymarks.

It's an interesting stroll for it takes you past some of the oldest and best of Les Haudères's buildings, then above the village a track

Les Haudères

continues at the same steady angle, soon among trees. When it bends sharply to the right leave the track for a path continuing straight ahead. When this forks take the upper, right-hand path which leads between meadows and onto the road near La Sage.

Almost immediately take a narrow tarmac road on the left. It winds between pastures and brings you up a slope to pass first Hotel de la Sage, then the village Post Office, before coming onto the road in the middle of **LA SAGE**[2] a few paces from Café-Restaurant L'Ecureuil.

> **LA SAGE** (1667m 4 hours) *Hotel, dortoir, restaurant, shop, PTT, Postbus. Office du Tourisme, 1985 La Sage* ☎ *(027) 283 12 80.*
>
> *Hotel de la Sage* ☎ *(027) 283 11 10 (pre-arranged groups only); dortoir at Café Restaurant L'Ecureuil* ☎ *(027) 283 11 38.*

Note: Limited (self-catering) accommodation is available at **VILLA** the next village along the road, about 15 minutes from La Sage. Apply at the small shop as you enter the village, or contact: Fam. Maurice Gaudin, 1985 Villa/La Sage ☎ *(027) 283 13 57.*

Places or Features of Interest Along the Way:

1: LES HAUDÈRES: This attractive, unspoilt and typically Valaisian village is mostly contained in a triangle delineated by two roads and a steep hillside at the head of Val d'Hérens. Most of its buildings are of timber on a stone base, with granaries mingled among the houses and small garden plots. Most of the houses are adorned with window boxes bursting with flowers, while the granaries, or hay barns, are perched on staddle stones to deter rodents. Les Haudères makes a good base for a walking holiday, the two adjacent valleys (of Arolla and Ferpècle) being of especial interest and with superb high mountain views.

2: LA SAGE: This small village is built on a natural terrace some 250 metres above the valley, with charming views across the head of the valley towards Pigne d'Arolla, or south-east to the snowfields and glaciers that spread between Dent Blanche and the Bouquetins ridge. A frequent Postbus service travels to and fro between Les Haudères and the roadhead at Villa, passing through La Sage. As with several other villages in the Val d'Hérens, local women often wear traditional long black dresses, decorated with colourful embroidery.

Distance:	**10 kilometres**
Time:	**5–5½ hours**
Start Altitude:	**1667m**
High point:	**Col du Tsaté 2868m**
Height gain:	**1617m**
Height loss:	**459m**
Map:	**L.S. 5006 Matterhorn–Mischabel 1:50,000 or L.S. 283T Arolla 1:50,000**
Accommodation:	**Cabane de Moiry – SAC refuge**
Transport options:	**None**
Alternative route:	**La Sage–Col de Torrent–Barrage de Moiry – see Alternative Stage 9**

*Between Val d'Hérens and Val d'Anniviers – the next major valley on
the journey heading east – lies the small but lovely Val de Moiry, a tributary glen that feeds Anniviers. A long ridge system which maintains
an altitude of 2900 metres and more extends north-westward from the
Grand Cornier, making an effective divide between the Vals d'Hérens
and Moiry, but with several accessible cols enabling walkers to cross
from one to the other.*

*Col du Tsaté is the lowest and most direct of these crossing points
for anyone staying in La Sage and planning to visit Cabane de Moiry,
while Col de Torrent further north will be the choice of walkers aiming
for either the dortoir at the Barrage de Moiry, or Grimentz.*

*The rocky Col du Tsaté forms a break in the ridge linking Pointe du
Bandon and the Couronne de Bréona, and although early Baedeker
guides spoke of it as being 'toilsome', there's nothing difficult about it –
a long, steep walk over grass slopes with an upper stony basin just
below the col, followed by an equally steep, but much shorter, descent
on the eastern side.*

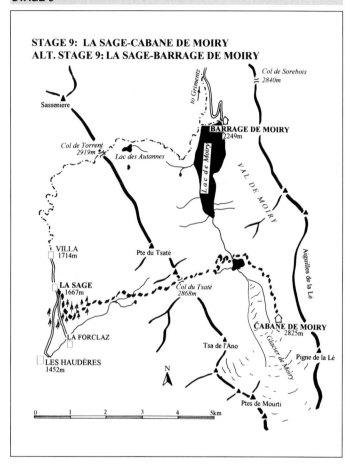

STAGE 9: LA SAGE-CABANE DE MOIRY
ALT. STAGE 9: LA SAGE-BARRAGE DE MOIRY

Sasseniere

Col de Torrent
2919m

Lac des Autannes

to Grimentz

Col de Sorebois
≈ 2840m

BARRAGE DE MOIRY
2249m

Lac de Moiry

VAL DE MOIRY

VILLA
1714m

Pte du Tsaté

LA SAGE
1667m

Col du Tsaté
2868m

LA FORCLAZ

Aiguilles de la Lé

CABANE DE MOIRY
2825m

LES HAUDÈRES
1452m

Tsa de l'Ano

Glacier de Moiry

Pigne de la Lé

N

Ptes de Mourti

0   1   2   3   4   5km

Cabane de Moiry stands on a rocky knoll overlooking the Moiry glacier in such a spectacular position that all effort to reach it will be considered worthwhile. The final approach to it climbs along a wall of lateral moraine, followed by a steep zig-zag path up rocks. It's quite a demanding route, but a rewarding one, and from the hut one gains an

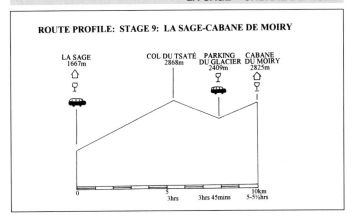

ROUTE PROFILE: STAGE 9: LA SAGE-CABANE DE MOIRY

amazing head-on view of the Moiry icefall. Of all lodgings on the Chamonix–Zermatt walk, this must rank among the finest for its setting.

From the centre of La Sage walk down the road in the direction of Les Haudères, and about 50 metres beyond Café-Restaurant L'Ecureuil bear left onto a track which rises easily into forest. After about 12 minutes you will come to the first of a few alp buildings, and shortly after turn a hairpin bend where another track breaks off to La Forclaz and Les Haudères. There will be several other alternatives above this, but the way to Col du Tsaté keeps to the main track rising among larchwoods. This eventually brings you to **MAYENS DE MOTAU** (1920m 35 mins), a small alp hamlet built on a steep open hillside enjoying fine views.

Above the hamlet the track stays close to a stream and narrows to a footpath which soon crosses to the left, then climbs again quite steeply alongside more larchwoods. After about 1 hour 10 mins come to another group of alp buildings, **LE TSATÉ** (2164m). Do not enter this hamlet, but continue uphill to cross a farm track and climb on up the steep hillside on a narrow path which leads to a solitary hut just below another section of unmade farm road (1½ hours).

Cross this road and take the path which slants leftward then zig-zags to gain height, before swinging to the right (south-east) and arriving at **REMOINTSE DU TSATÉ** (2480m 1 hour 50 mins) – two long cowsheds and a small dairyman's hut. These buildings are situated at the entrance to a grass basin in which there's a small tarn. The continuing path slants across the left-hand hillside overlooking the tarn, then curves leftwards to climb to a second basin where the way forks. Keep with the right-hand option, rising to a crucifix at the entrance to a third and final basin – this one much more austere and stony than the last, at the head of which is Col du Tsaté.

Passing just to the right of the crucifix the path crosses the stony bed of the valley, then rises on the left-hand walling hillside. As height is gained the way grows progressively more rocky until at last you emerge onto the summit of **COL DU TSATÉ** (2868m 2¾–3 hours).

The east side of the ridge which falls to the Val de Moiry[1] is also stony at first, and the descent steep in places as it crosses screes and slopes of shale before coming onto a pleasant grass shelf (about 20 minutes below the col) from which you gain a first view of the Moiry icefall[2] and refuge – this stands atop rock slabs to the left of the icefall. Continue down to a small tarn and a path junction (2547m).

Note: The *Haut Tour du Lac/Chemin 2500m* makes a traverse left, and joins the route of Alternative Stage 9 at a farm, Alpage de Torrent. Should you have changed your mind about going to the Moiry refuge, you could follow this path to the farm, then descend to the Barrage de Moiry for overnight in a *dortoir*.

In order to continue to the Cabane take the path ahead, signed to Parking du Glacier. It descends in zig-zags, now with the dammed Lac de Moiry seen to the north, and eventually brings you to a track which swings down to the roadhead **PARKING DU GLACIER** (2409m 3 hours 45 mins) which has a small *buvette* (refreshment hut) and a bus stop for Grimentz.

Pass to the left of the *buvette* onto a track signed to Cabane de Moiry. The track soon becomes a footpath which rises onto the east side lateral moraine walling the Moiry glacier. After picking a way along the narrow moraine crest it slopes down into the little ablation valley before climbing in zig-zags up rocky slopes which lead directly to the **CABANE DE MOIRY**.[3]

CABANE DE MOIRY (2825m 5–5½ hours) *108 places, full meals service when the guardian is present – end of June to end of September.* ☎ *(027) 475 45 34.*

Places or Features of Interest Along the Way:

1: VAL DE MOIRY: This small glen feeds into the longer Val d'Anniviers, of which it forms the south-western tributary. It rises in a wedge of peaks whose nodal point is the Grand Cornier (3962m), and in whose upper ridges a basin of névé gives birth to the Moiry glacier. Below the glacier two small tarns are used as settlement reservoirs to reduce the flow of glacial silt into the larger dammed Lac de Moiry below. Along the hillsides east and west of the lake a very fine path has been created more or less following the 2500 metre contour, and is promoted as the Haut Tour du Lac, from which the full extent of the valley is on display (a 5-hour circuit). Below the Barrage de Moiry the glen is somewhat wild, but it becomes green and wooded towards Grimentz, an attractive village near the valley mouth and the only one in Val de Moiry. In summer a frequent Postbus service runs between Grimentz and Parking du Glacier. At the barrage there's a restaurant, with a linking *dortoir* just above on the east side of the dam.

2: THE MOIRY ICEFALL: The icefall of the Moiry glacier is among the most impressive of its kind in the Pennine Alps, and that the mountain walker can gaze upon it from so close and safe a vantage point as the hut, makes it extra special. In *The Alps in 1864*, the Victorian pioneer A W Moore wrote about it in glowing terms, referring to it as: "...a tremendous ice-fall of great height and very steep. The lower part ... extends completely from one side of the glacier to the other, but higher up, under the Pigne de la Lex, is a belt of smooth ice, which we had no doubt would give access to the field of névé above the fall. Below this great cascade of séracs, the ice is as compact and level as above it is steep and dislocated. Indeed, I never saw an ice-fall confined within such plainly defined limits, or terminate so abruptly."

3: CABANE DE MOIRY: Owned by the Montreux section of the Swiss Alpine Club, the Moiry hut is built in a dramatic location among a horseshoe of peaks and glaciers. Above it to the east runs the wall of the Aiguilles de la Lé; opposite rise Couronne de Bréona, Pointe de Moiry and Tsa de l'Ano. Between the Couronne and Pointe de Moiry lies the Col de Couronne by which access to the glen may be achieved from the head of Val d'Hérens (a more strenuous and less well-marked route than either Col du Tsaté or Col de Torrent), while south-east of the hut, between the last of the Aiguilles de la Lé and Pigne de la Lé,

The Cabane de Moiry

Col du Pigne offers another way over to Zinal. (Not for inexperienced mountain walkers though.) The hut is popular among ski-mountaineers, for several of the summits that enclose the glacier provide enjoyable ski ascents. Pigne de la Lé and Pointe de Bricola (north-west of Grand Cornier) are among the most popular, while summer ascents are made directly from the hut to Grand Cornier and all the neighbouring peaks. By virtue of its short approach from the roadhead (1½ hours), Cabane de Moiry receives plenty of day-visitors.

LA SAGE – COL DE TORRENT – BARRAGE DE MOIRY/GRIMENTZ

Distance:	10 kilometres
Time:	5 hours
Start altitude:	1667m
High point:	Col de Torrent 2919m
Height gain:	1252m
Height loss:	670m
Map:	L.S. 5006 Matterhorn–Mischabel 1:50,000 or L.S. 283T Arolla 1:50,000
Accommodation:	Villa (15 mins) – self-catering rooms Chalet du Barrage – *dortoir*
Transport options:	Postbus (Barrage de Moiry–Grimentz)
Alternative routes:	i] Barrage de Moiry to Grimentz – see below ii] to Cabane de Moiry via Col du Tsaté – see Stage 9

A little over 4 kilometres north-west of Col du Tsaté (crossed on Stage 9 above) the higher Col de Torrent is a popular and much-used link between the Vals d'Hérens and Moiry. Pastureland rises almost all the way to the col on both sides of the ridge, and views are consistently fine. The way up to the pass is a delight, while the panorama on the eastern side is the equal of almost anything seen so far, and descent to the dammed Lac de Moiry is both undemanding and visually rewarding.

The dortoir above the barrage is ideally placed for the crossing of Col de Sorebois to Zinal next day, but some commercial trekking parties (and a few individuals) choose not stay at the Chalet du Barrage, continuing instead down to Grimentz where there's a range of accommodation on offer. With this option the onward route misses Zinal completely by going directly to Hotel Weisshorn, thereby reducing the

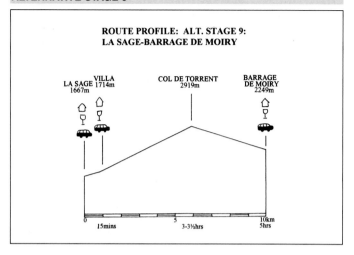

ROUTE PROFILE: ALT. STAGE 9:
LA SAGE-BARRAGE DE MOIRY

length of the walk by one day. Brief details of this option are given below.

Walk up the road from La Sage to **VILLA** (1714m 15 mins, *accommodation, refreshments, shop, Postbus*). Just across the bridge in Villa come to a small white chapel on the left of the road. Turn immediately opposite this to walk between two granaries on the right, and then head uphill on a cobbled track. The cobbles run out at the upper end of the village but a track continues. A footpath then leads on to climb the steeply sloping hillside.

From the outset views are grand, not just to those peaks behind that have grown familiar from walking beside them during the past few days, but ahead too, to mountains of the Bernese Alps on the far side of the Rhône valley. Les Diablerets and the Wildhorn massif look especially appealing.

The path brings you to a track beyond a small chalet. Turn right here, but round the next bend where the track forks take the left-hand branch. This winds between pastures and leads to an alp hamlet and yet another track (2160m). Bear left, and in a few paces take a rising path on the right above a water trough.

Gaining height, sometimes steeply, you pass below a small isolated hut near some pillars of upstanding rock. This is **BEPLAN** (2486m 1 hour 45 mins). The trail winds round to the right where you enter a high alp pasture with another hut seen off to the left. Soon come to a small pond (2536m), from which Col de Torrent appears as a modest saddle above to the right. Wandering up in long loops, steeply now and then over high pastures, the way at last emerges onto **COL DE TORRENT** (2919m 3–3½ hours).

Views from the col are tremendous. To south and west the panorama includes the Mont Miné, Tête Blanche, Grande Dent de Veisivi, Mont Brulé, Pigne d'Arolla, Mont Blanc de Cheilon, Grand Combin, the Aiguilles Rouges, Rosablanche and the Grand Désert glacier, and far off the snowy mass of Mont Blanc. Turning to the east across the lovely Lac des Autannes and jade-green Lac de Moiry which lie in the deep trough of Val de Moiry – across the far ridge that walls it – stand Weisshorn, Schalihorn and Pointe Sud de Moming.

Note: For an even broader panorama than that won from the col, go left up the ridge for 45 minutes (allow 1½ hours for the round-trip) to the summit of Sasseneire (3250m) – far to the north you can just make out the line of the Jura through the Col de Cheville, while to the south the Dent Blanche, which is not seen from the Col de Torrent, dominates the view.

A clear path descends on the Moiry side, first heading north, then swinging eastward down to undulating pastures. As you draw level with the picturesque Lac des Autannes, some 230 metres or so below the col, exquisite views are to be had across the tarn to a turmoil of glaciers and the peaks which block the head of Val de Moiry. Up there, Pigne de la Lé and Grand Cornier cast ridges, snowfields and long streamers of ice, creating those contrasts of light and shade, height and depth, barren upland against a foreground of soft pasture, that make wandering in the Alps such a memorable experience.

On coming to a farm (**ALPAGE DE TORRENT** 2481m) the route of the Haut Tour du Lac/Chemin 2500 breaks off to the right. The way to the barrage, however, continues ahead.

Note: Should you change your mind and decide to visit Cabane de Moiry as per the main route, follow this right-hand path across the hillside until you reach a small tarn and a trail junction. Turn left and descend to Parking du Moiry at the roadhead, then follow the route to the Cabane as described in Stage 9.

The descending track loops down to the massive **BARRAGE DE**

MOIRY (2249m) at the northern end of Lac de Moiry. Cross the dam to a restaurant on the eastern side (5 hours *refreshments, w.c., public telephone, Postbus to Grimentz*). For *dortoir* accommodation apply at the restaurant. The *dortoir*, Chalet du Barrage, stands a little higher above the road (☎ *(027) 475 15 48; 26 places, open June–October*).

Note i: Walkers intending to visit Grimentz for overnight accommodation should take the left-hand path on the western side of the barrage. This slants along the hillside, descends to the road and continues to:

GRIMENTZ (1572m 6½–7 hours) *Accommodation, refreshments, shops, bank, PTT, Postbus (to Zinal, St Luc, Vissoie, Sierre, etc). Office du Tourisme, 3961 Grimentz* ☎ *(027) 475 14 93.*

Lower-priced hotels: Chalet Bouquetin ☎ *(027) 475 17 88; Le Meleze* ☎ *(027) 475 12 87; Hotel de Moiry* ☎ *(027) 475 11 44.*

Note ii: There are three optional onward routes from Grimentz: i] take the Postbus back to the **BARRAGE DE MOIRY** and follow the signed path to Col de Sorebois and Zinal as described in Stage 10 below; ii] follow the waymarked route from Grimentz to **ZINAL** (2½ hours) where you rejoin the main Chamonix to Zermatt walk at the start of Stage 11; iii] take a signed route on footpaths and tracks to Mission (30 mins) and then quite steeply uphill to **HOTEL WEISSHORN** (described at the end of Alternative Stage 11) in about 4 hours from Grimentz.

STAGE 10:

CABANE DE MOIRY – COL DE SOREBOIS- ZINAL

Distance:	**14 kilometres**
Time:	**5–5½ hours**
Start altitude:	**2825m**
High point:	**Col de Sorebois c2840m**
Height gain:	**455m**
Height loss:	**1605m**
Maps:	**L.S. 5006 Matterhorn–Mischabel 1:50,000 or L.S. 283T Arolla & 273T Montana 1:50,000**
Accommodation:	**Cabane de Sorebois (3¾ hours) –** *dortoir* **Zinal – hotels,** *dortoir,* **camping**
Transport options:	**Postbus (Barrage de Moiry–Grimentz–Zinal) Cable-car (Sorebois–Zinal)**

This stage, leading from the arctic splendour of the upper Val de Moiry to the deep forested trench of Val de Zinal (the upper reaches of Val d'Anniviers) entails the crossing of yet another high ridge. This time, however, the effort required to reach it is not unduly fatiguing, while the panorama that greets you on arrival at Col de Sorebois is truly memorable, with Weisshorn and Zinalrothorn on show almost all the way down to Zinal.

After descending along the moraine wall below Cabane de Moiry, a superb belvedere trail carries the route along the hillside heading north about 300 metres above Lac de Moiry. The hillside is noted for its alpine flowers, and there's also a good chance of catching sight of chamois or even ibex. When the contouring path meets a track above the barrage, our route breaks off to the right and climbs easily to Col de Sorebois. But the toughest part of the day is reserved for the final descent into Zinal – an extremely steep forest path that will aggravate tired knees.

Stayed in Grimentz, Bus to St. Luc

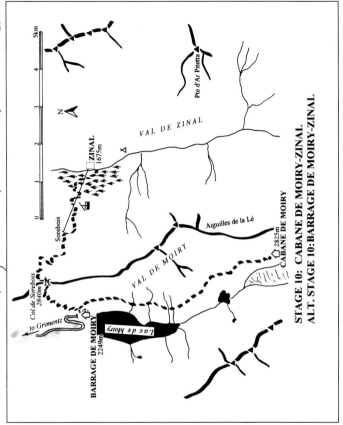

STAGE 10: CABANE DE MOIRY–ZINAL
ALT. STAGE 10: BARRAGE DE MOIRY–ZINAL

Descend from the hut on the same path used for the approach, and after about 45 minutes, when you've left the moraine bank and the path becomes wider and easier at an altitude of about 2150 metres, a path breaks off to the right signed to Barrage de Moiry, Col de Sorebois, Zinal–Grimentz. This path which forms part of the Haut Tour du Lac (the Chemin 2500m) follows a fairly regular contour across the grassy hillside. About 15 minutes along this path come to a junction where

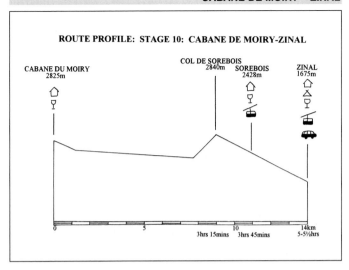

ROUTE PROFILE: STAGE 10: CABANE DE MOIRY-ZINAL

CABANE DU MOIRY
2825m

COL DE SOREBOIS
2840m

SOREBOIS
2428m

ZINAL
1675m

0

5

10

14km

3hrs 15mins   3hrs 45mins

5-5½hrs

the left-hand option descends to the roadhead car park; the way to Col de Sorebois continues ahead.

It's a very fine path offering splendid views of the glacial landscape you've left behind, and after a while overlooks the jade-green waters of Lac de Moiry and the valley falling away in the distance.

Towards the end of the lake the path slopes downhill to meet a junction of grass tracks (2385m 2 hours 15 mins). Continue ahead, ignoring the lower route to the Barrage de Moiry, and begin rising in long loops. Soon after making a right-hand hairpin note a waymarked path rising on the left – this is the path to take for the Col de Sorebois. It becomes more established as you gain height – sometimes quite steeply with zig-zags. Views are mostly down-valley towards Grimentz. There is a good possibility of catching sight of chamois and marmots on the way to the pass.

Come onto the saddle of **COL DE SOREBOIS** (c2840m 3 hours 15 mins) where you will find a signpost – the altitude marked as 2896m is wrong; this refers to Corne de Sorebois at the head of the ridge to the left. But of more interest than the times and destinations shown on the sign is the incredible panorama of high peaks opposite, dominated by the Weisshorn.[1] Ignore if you can the reshaped ski terrain below and enjoy one of the finest views so far. Though hard to believe, it's a view that improves as you descend.

For the descent into Val de Zinal,[2] first bear left and rise a short way along the ridge, then slant right on a track/ski piste that sweeps down in long windings to the **SOREBOIS** cableway station (2438m 3 hours 45 mins; *dortoir accommodation, refreshments, cable-car to Zinal*).

Bear right along a track for a short distance, then take a signposted track/path that winds down in zig-zags with plenty of waymarks, cutting to and fro beneath the cableway, then entering forest where the path becomes even steeper – something of a knee-jarring descent. The path is clear and obvious and it eventually brings you to a footbridge over the Navisence torrent and up into **ZINAL**.[3]

> **ZINAL** (1675m 5–5½ hours) *Accommodation, camping, restaurants, shops, bank, PTT, Postbus (Zinal–Vissoie–St Luc–Sierre). Office du Tourisme, 3961 Zinal* ☎ *(027) 475 31 65.*
>
> *Lower-priced accommodation: Auberge Alpina (dortoir & rooms)* ☎ *(027) 475 12 24 – open 15 June – 15 Oct; Hotel Le Trift* ☎ *(027) 475 14 66; Hotel de la Poste* ☎ *(027) 475 11 87; Hotel A La Pointe* ☎ *(027) 475 11 64.*
>
> Note: *The proprietor at Auberge Alpina also has two chalets with kitchen facilities for rent. Telephone number as above, or fax: (027) 475 50 33.*

Places or Features of Interest Along the Way:

1: THE WEISSHORN: A beautiful mountain with three faces and three ridges, at 4505 metres it ranks as one of the highest in the Pennine Alps (the second highest standing solely in Switzerland). Forming part of that great ridge which separates Val de Zinal from the Mattertal, the Weisshorn is eye-catching from several different angles, and by the time you reach Zermatt you will have grown very familiar with it. As a mountaineer's mountain the main interest lies in its ridges, and it was by way of the East Ridge that it received its first ascent on 19 August 1861 by the pioneering Victorian scientist and mountaineer John Tyndall (1820–93), with J J Bennen and Ulrich Wenger as his guides.

2: VAL DE ZINAL: The name given to the upper reaches of Val d'Anniviers, Val de Zinal holds much of interest to both walkers and

Alpine pasture, Sorebois, above Val de Zinal

climbers. Indeed, some of the most varied and scenically spectacular walks of the whole Pennine Alps chain are to be enjoyed here, while the big peaks that wall it hold some dramatic routes. The head of the valley is a spectacular amphitheatre of ice and snow with Ober Gabelhorn, Mont Durand, Pointe de Zinal, Dent Blanche, Grand Cornier and the Bouquetins rising from it. Zinalrothorn, Pointe Sud de Moming, Schalihorn and Weisshorn create another cirque in the southeast, while opposite this the pasture bowl of La Lé is backed by another rocky crescent. Evidence of past glaciations can be read quite clearly within the valley itself. For a selection of walks in and around the valley, see *The Valais*, a walking guide published by Cicerone Press.

3: ZINAL: This long-time mountaineering centre is steadily growing at its northern end. The original village, crowded with timber houses and granaries, forms an attractive line along the true right bank of the valley between the 'new' village and the campsite. Zinal is the final settlement in the long Val d'Anniviers; beyond it the valley grows increasingly wild and austere with glaciers, moraine banks and a glorious array of high mountains. Although the majority of walks here entail some pretty steep ascents and descents, Zinal makes an excellent base for a walking or climbing holiday.

ALTERNATIVE STAGE 10:

BARRAGE DE MOIRY –
COL DE SOREBOIS – ZINAL

Distance:	8 kilometres
Time:	4–4½ hours
Start altitude:	2249m
High point:	Col de Sorebois c2840m
Height gain:	591m
Height loss:	1165m
Maps:	L.S. 5006 Matterhorn–Mischabel 1:50,000 or L.S. 283T Arolla & 273T Montana 1:50,000
Accommodation:	Cabane de Sorebois (2¾ hours) – *dortoir* Zinal – hotels, *dortoir*, camping
Transport options:	Postbus (Barrage de Moiry–Grimentz–Zinal) Cable-car (Sorebois–Zinal)
Alternative routes:	Barrage de Moiry to Zinal or Hotel Weisshorn via Grimentz – see details at end of Alternative Stage 9

An easy and straightforward crossing of Col de Sorebois takes the C–Z trekker into the lovely Val de Zinal among the highest mountains of the route since leaving the Mont Blanc massif. On the ascent to the pass there's a distinct possibility of seeing chamois and marmots, while the view from the col itself is awe-inspiring.

From the *dortoir* just above the Barrage de Moiry wander up the track to the junction with the route of the Haut Tour du Lac (which breaks to the right), then continue uphill in long loops until after making a right-hand hairpin you cut off on a narrow waymarked path rising on the left. This leads eventually to Col de Sorebois, on occasion with steep zig-zags and long views down-valley towards Grimentz.

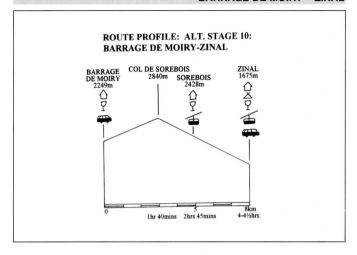

ROUTE PROFILE: ALT. STAGE 10:
BARRAGE DE MOIRY-ZINAL

You should gain the easy saddle of **COL DE SOREBOIS** (c2840m) after about 1 hour 40 minutes. (Ignore the altitude marked on the sign-post, which refers to the high point of Corne de Sorebois off to the left: 2896m). A magnificent panorama of high peaks, dominated by the Weisshorn, greets you on arrival.

Bear left and rise for a short distance along the ridge, then slant down to the right on a track/ski piste that sweeps in long windings to the cable-car station of **SOREBOIS** (2438m 2 hours 45 mins *accommodation, refreshments, cable-car to Zinal*). Bear right along a track for a few minutes, then take a signposted track/path off to the left.

Note: A longer, but more interesting and visually rewarding descent, taking another 3½ hours from here, continues along the track and takes signed footpaths to Alp La Lé and Cabane du Petit Mountet (2142m *accommodation, refreshments* ☎ (027) 475 10 89), before cutting back down to Zinal which the path reaches at the southern end of the village by the campsite.

The direct route down to Zinal is adequately waymarked and signed after turning off from the track south of the Sorebois cable-car station. After crossing a gently sloping pasture, the path zig-zags down-hill for some way before slanting beneath the cableway and entering forest. Here the gradient steepens and the path becomes something of a knee-jarring descent until eventually it eases down to a footbridge that takes you across the river and up into **ZINAL**.

ZINAL (1675m 4–4½ hours) *Accommodation, camping, restaurants, shops, bank, PTT, Postbus (Zinal–Vissoie–St Luc–Sierre). Office du Tourisme, 3961 Zinal* ☎ *(027) 475 31 65.*

Lower-priced accommodation: Auberge Alpina (dortoir & rooms) ☎ *(027) 475 12 24 – open 15 June – 15 Oct; Hotel Le Trift* ☎ *(027) 475 14 66; Hotel de la Poste* ☎ *(027) 475 11 87; Hotel A La Pointe* ☎ *(027) 475 11 64.*

Note: *The proprietor at Auberge Alpina also has two chalets with kitchen facilities for rent. Telephone number as above, or fax: (027) 475 50 33.*

STAGE 11:

ZINAL – FORCLETTA – GRUBEN

Distance:	**14 kilometres**
Time:	**5½–6 hours**
Start altitude:	**1675m**
High point:	**Forcletta 2874m**
Height gain:	**1199m**
Height loss:	**1052m**
Maps:	**L.S. 5006 Matterhorn–Mischabel 1:50,000 or L.S. 283T Arolla, 273T Montana & 274T Visp 1:50,000**
Accommodation:	**Gruben – hotel (beds &** *matratzenlager/ dortoir*) **and inn (***matratzenlager***)**
Transport options:	**None**
Alternative route:	**Zinal–Hotel Weisshorn – see Alternative Stage 11, & Hotel Weisshorn–Meidpass– Gruben (Alternative Stage 11a)**

The next valley on the eastward route is the little-known Turtmanntal, with Gruben (otherwise known as Meiden) being the first German-speaking community of the walk. It's a lovely half-forgotten back-water, for the valley is occupied only in summer. Not long after the cattle have been taken down to farms in lowland Switzerland, Gruben closes up until the following spring.

There are two main ways of reaching the Turtmanntal from Zinal: via the Forcletta as per this stage, and over the Meidpass via Hotel Weisshorn as described under Alternative Stages 11 and 11a. Both are fine crossings, but the Forcletta has the edge – as well as being the more direct, it also provides the best scenic attractions. In short, it is a magnificent crossing, despite missing the opportunity of staying overnight in Hotel Weisshorn – a memorable experience and, to many,

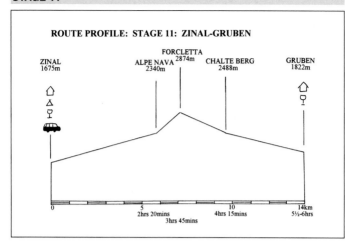

ROUTE PROFILE: STAGE 11: ZINAL-GRUBEN

a highlight of the Walker's Haute Route. (A way of combining a night in Hotel Weisshorn with a crossing of the Forcletta is given in Alternative Stage 11a.)

The Zinal tourist office is situated at the northern entrance to the village. A minor road slants uphill just behind it, and this is the start of the walk – a sign announces Barneuza Alpage (1 hour 50 mins) and Hotel Weisshorn (3 hours). Follow the road round to the left to pass La Versache Creperie & Café. Continuing, the way swings back to the right and takes you above the first of Zinal's buildings. Immediately past a large apartment block turn left on a service road (sign to Hotel Weisshorn) which takes you between buildings, left towards a parking area, then right on a rising track among larch trees. Go through a tunnel and across an avalanche defence system.

Once across this the path, which is broad and well-trodden, begins to make height in the forest, and by a series of steep zig-zags soon takes you high above the valley. About 50 minutes from Zinal the gradient eases into a more gently rising traverse, and an hour from the start you come out of the trees and onto an open hillside shelf (2173m) with a charming backward view to Pigne de la Lé, Grand Cornier and Dent Blanche, while ahead you gaze across the Rhône valley to the line of the Bernese Alps.

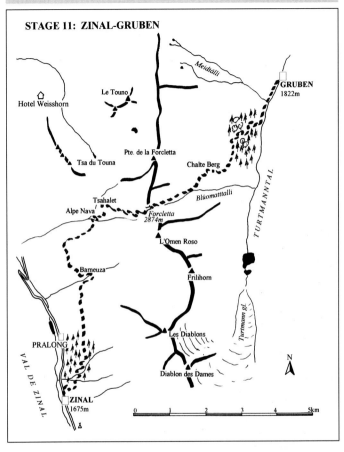

STAGE 11: ZINAL-GRUBEN

Meidtälli

☐ **GRUBEN**
1822m

☐ Hotel Weisshorn

Le Touno

Tsa du Touna

Pte. de la Forcletta

Chalte Berg

Blüomatttalli

Tsahalet

Alpe Nava

Forcletta
2874m

L'Omen Roso

TURTMANNTAL

Barneuza

Frilihorn

Turtmann gl.

☐ PRALONG

Les Diablons

N

V A L   D E   Z I N A L

Diablon des Dames

☐ **ZINAL**
1675m

0   1   2   3   4   5km

The path now develops into a superb belvedere heading north along the hillside, and in due course you will come to the isolated farm of **BARNEUZA ALPAGE** (2211m 1 hour 45 mins). Immediately beyond the alp buildings there's a junction of paths. One is signed to Mission, Les Moyes, etc; another to Col Arettes and Remointse, but the trail to take is that which is marked to Hotel Weisshorn – the upper path rising ahead.

Eventually this turns a spur and cuts into a deep combe. Immediately after crossing a stream you come to a solitary semi-derelict hut, **ALPE NAVA** (2340m 2 hours 20 mins). A few paces beyond this there's another signed junction. Take that which climbs to the right (direction Forcletta and Gruben). It rises over grass slopes drained by a stream, is faint in places, but with sufficient red–white waymarks to direct the way.

Skirting the right-hand slope of a pastureland bowl enter an upper level and bear left, then rise to an alp (**TSAHALET** 2523m) marked by a large wooden cross. This is reached about 20 minutes from Alpe Nava.

At the right-hand end of the cattle sheds waymarks direct the continuing path across a rucked and pitted grassland, on the far side of which a clear path takes you up rocky slopes. The way climbs easily in long zig-zags to gain the **FORCLETTA** (2874m 3 hours 45 mins), a bare saddle in a ridge stubbed with individual peaklets. Ahead lies the glen of Blüomatttalli which appears stony and barren – although as you descend through it, you will discover it is full of alpine plants. Looking back from the pass long distant views include the Aiguilles Rouges above Arolla.

Slant left across a slope of shale, then ease down the left-hand side of the shallow Blüomatttalli where a stream drains between great cushions of moss and flowering plants. Towards the lower end of the glen the Brunegghorn comes into view to the right across the Turtmanntal,[1] then its long glacier with the Bishorn looking huge to the right of that, and the graceful north ridge of the Weisshorn[2] rising above the Bishorn. "I doubt whether there is a more spiky panorama to be seen in the Alps than this view across the Turtmanntal from the Forcletta descent," wrote Showell Styles in *Backpacking in the Alps and Pyrenees*.

The path now veers left over rolling pastures and slopes down to the farm buildings of **CHALTE BERG** (2488m 4 hours 15 mins). Views of the Bishorn, Weisshorn and the snow crest leading to the Tête de Milon are tremendous from here.

Pass between the alp buildings where the route is guided by waymarks directly down the grass slope beyond the alp to an unmade farm road. Turn left along it, and after about 150 metres bear right on a footpath which descends a little, then runs parallel to the road, later dropping well below it to more alp huts (**MASSSTAFEL** 2235m). The path brings you onto the road once more and you turn right along it

Barneuza Alp, high above the Val de Zinal

for a short distance, then find the continuing path on the right, directly opposite the last hut. This soon brings you onto the road yet again.

Note: There are two routes down to Gruben: i] starting at a hairpin bend just above where you come onto the road, this option makes a long traverse across the hillside to Mittel Stafel where it joins the route from Meidpass (Alternative Stage 11a) to descend to Gruben; ii] a shorter, recommended option crosses the road and turns right to descend below it – described as follows.

Cross the road onto the path which descends below it, soon to enter forest where the way zig-zags down. At times the undergrowth beside the path crowds the way, although there's nothing difficult about the descent. This finally brings you to the valley bed by more farm buildings about 1 kilometre above Gruben.

Walk towards the valley road, but do not cross the Turtmänna river. Instead take a faint grass path on the left bank and follow this downstream towards Gruben, eventually coming to a path junction near two chalets. Turn right, cross the river and enter **GRUBEN**.[3]

GRUBEN (MEIDEN) (1822m 5½–6 hours) *Accommodation, refreshments, shop.*

Hotel Schwarzhorn (beds & matratzenlager) ☎ *(027) 932 14 14 – open June to October; Restaurant Waldesruh (5 minutes down-valley; matratzenlager)* ☎ *(027) 932 13 97 – open mid-June to mid-September.*

Places or Features of Interest Along the Way:

1: THE TURTMANNTAL: This is one of the shortest valleys in the Pennine Alps, and one of the least developed. Access from the Rhône valley is by a steeply twisting road via Oberems, but unusually for Switzerland there is no Postbus service above that village. The valley itself rises in the south where the combined ridges of Brunegghorn, Bishorn and Tête de Milon form a lofty wall that never drops below 3500 metres. (The Weisshorn rises above and to the south of Bishorn and Tête de Milon.) Both the Turtmann and Brunegg glaciers sweep down from this wall and weld together beneath Les Diablons. Below this junction, on the right bank of the glacier, stands the Turtmann Hut (2520m 50 places, 3 hours from Gruben), base for climbs on such peaks as the Tête de Milon, Bishorn, Brunegghorn and Barrhorn, the latter having a tremendous view of the Mattertal and the Mischabel peaks opposite. The valley is completely pastoral with a number of farms and small hamlets. Cattle graze the lower pastures, sheep roam higher on the hillsides.

2: THE WEISSHORN: Yet again this graceful mountain announces its looming presence. In his classic book *The Playground of Europe* Leslie Stephen wrote of the view from just outside Gruben: "Above us rose the Weisshorn in one of the most sublime aspects of that almost fault-less mountain. The Turtmann glacier, broad and white with deep regular crevasses, formed a noble approach, like the staircase of some superb palace. Above this rose the huge mass of the mountain, firm and solid as though its architect wished to eclipse the Pyramids. And, higher still, its lofty crest, jagged and apparently swaying from side to side, seemed to be tossed into the blue atmosphere far above the reach of mortal man. Nowhere have I seen a more delicate combination of mountain massiveness, with soaring and delicately carved pinnacles pushed to the verge of extravagence. Yet few people know of this side of a peak, which every one has admired from the Riffel [above Zermatt]."

Gruben in the Turtmanntal

3: GRUBEN: Also known as Meiden, this small village ("more like a Swiss village of the Golden Age of Mountaineering than any other" according to Showell Styles) is the only one in the valley proper – Oberems and Unterems are at the entrance. It consists of a neat cluster of houses, trim white chapel and hotel above flood-level on the right bank of the Turtmänna stream, idyllically placed between the Meidpass and Augstbordpass by which you leave the valley on the Walker's Haute Route. The small store near Hotel Schwarzhorn stocks a surprising variety of goods. About 500 metres down-valley from the main village stands the rustic Restaurant Waldesruh. For a time it served as a children's home, then was converted to a youth hostel. It is now a licensed restaurant with *matratzenlager* accommodation on the second floor.

ALTERNATIVE STAGE 11:

ZINAL – HOTEL WEISSHORN

Distance:	**10 kilometres**
Time:	**3½–4 hours**
Start altitude:	**1675m**
High point:	**Montagne de Nava 2400m**
Height gain:	**725m**
Height loss:	**63m**
Map:	**L.S. 5006 Matterhorn–Mischabel 1:50,000 or L.S. 283T Arolla & 273T Montana 1:50,000**
Accommodation:	**Hotel Weisshorn (beds & *dortoir*)**
Transport options:	**None**
Alternative route:	**Zinal to Gruben via the Forcletta – see Stage 11**

The path which runs along a high shelf of hillside on the east wall of Val d'Anniviers between Zinal and Hotel Weisshorn provides one of the great walks of Switzerland, and presents such stunning views to the head of the valley that you will probably wish it were possible to walk backwards! The magic of the upper Val d'Anniviers (Val de Zinal) with its crowded mass of snow and ice giants makes this an alpine wonderland, and in order to absorb as much of that magic as possible will inevitably result in the day's walk taking a lot longer than the basic four hours quoted above.

As for Hotel Weisshorn, this large Victorian building lost some of its former eccentricity when it was refurbished a few years ago, but the charm remains, as does the surprise of its setting. A night spent there is counted among the highlights of the Chamonix to Zermatt walk by a large number of trekkers. Advanced booking recommended – see details at the end of this section.

Autumn mist in the valley below Jungen (Stage 12)

The Weisshorn dominates the early stages of the Europaweg (Stage 13)

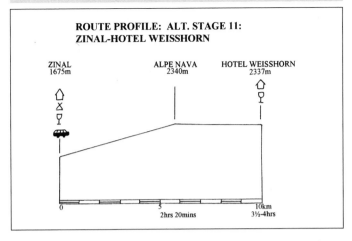

**ROUTE PROFILE: ALT. STAGE 11:
ZINAL-HOTEL WEISSHORN**

Follow directions given in Stage 11 (Zinal–Forcletta–Gruben) as far as
ALPE NAVA (2340m 2 hours 20 mins). Ignore the minor path breaking
off to the right (to the Forcletta) and continue ahead – the sign here
gives 1 hour to Hotel Weisshorn. On this section of the walk the
southern panorama grows even more impressive and includes the
Zinalrothorn, the upper chisel-shaped summit of the Matterhorn, Dent
Blanche, etc, and it's worth having plenty of halts to enjoy these views.

*We were on course for setting a record for the slowest-ever walk
from Zinal to Hotel Weisshorn. Our day had become like Morse
code, a succession of dots and dashes as we stumbled along the
path among autumn-tinged bilberry leaves now blazing scarlet.
Progress was painfully slow, for we had to keep turning to where
the southern horizon was an upthrust of spires and domes, a patch-
work of grey rock and unmarked snow, of gleaming ice and deep
blue shadow. Down below the valley had been brushed with early
frost that sparkled as it turned to moisture. Now vegetation had
dried in the sunlight, and dark swathes of forest lapped against the
lower hillside. Bare grass textured the upper levels with velvet.
Then rock, and snow and ice appeared far off. The head of the
valley was the birthplace of glaciers, and all down Val d'Anniviers
we could see a tribute to their industry. It was all too good to
ignore, and there could be no haste to this day.*

St. Luc

Funicular

ALT. STAGE 11: ZINAL-HOTEL WEISSHORN
ALT. STAGE 11a: HOTEL WEISSHORN-GRUBEN

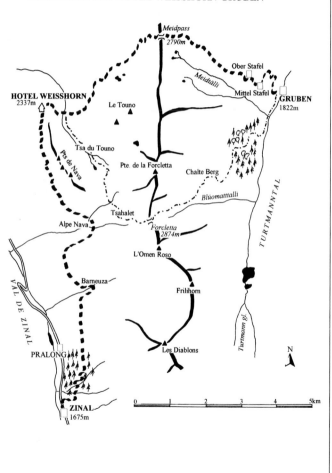

All this route between Zinal and Hotel Weisshorn is part of a mountain marathon[1] course that takes place each summer. The yellow-painted letter Z which appears at many junctions is a route guide for this marathon.

Rising still you join a track and continue ahead on a footpath running parallel with it, but at a higher level. (The track winds down to Ayer; the footpath is marked to St Luc.) On coming to a second track by some avalanche defences bear left along it, and shortly after take the rising path ahead.

The trail rises and falls across an undulating hillside and soon brings you in sight of Hotel Weisshorn, while an interesting mountain basin is seen off to the right. Just above the hotel join a track and bear left down it to reach **HOTEL WEISSHORN**.[2]

HOTEL WEISSHORN (2337m 3½–4 hours) *beds & dortoir, restaurant service – open June to mid-October. Contact: Hotel Weisshorn, 3961 St Luc* ☎ *(027) 475 11 06 – Reservation recommended.*

Note: Should you fail to gain accommodation here, try Cabane Bella-Tola (2346m) which is less than an hour's walk to the north. *Cabane Bella Tola, 120 places, meals provided, open July–Sept* ☎ *(027) 475 15 37.*

Places or Features of Interest Along the Way:

1: MOUNTAIN MARATHON: Every summer a mountain marathon takes place between Sierre in the Rhône valley and Zinal. Not only is it the full marathon distance of over 26 miles (42km), the amount of height gain is impressive. Sierre lies at around 550 metres above sea level, while sections of the path between Hotel Weisshorn and Zinal are at more than 2400 metres.

2: HOTEL WEISSHORN: This large, imposing building which dates from the 1880s is almost an institution. Set in a magnificent position more than a thousand metres above the valley bed, it has the Rhône valley to the north with the chain of the Bernese Alps rising above that. Sunset views are especially fine. The hotel is open from June to mid-October, and from Christmas to mid-April, and is popular for wedding parties and other celebrations.

ALTERNATIVE STAGE 11a:

HOTEL WEISSHORN – MEIDPASS – GRUBEN

Distance:	**9 kilometres**
Time:	**4 hours**
Start altitude:	**2337m**
High point:	**Meidpass 2790m**
Height gain:	**589m**
Height loss:	**1104m**
Maps:	**L.S. 5006 Matterhorn–Mischabel 1:50,000 or L.S. 283T Arolla, 273T Montana & 274T Visp 1:50,000**
Accommodation:	**Gruben – hotel (beds & *matratzenlager/ dortoir*) and inn (*matratzenlager*)**
Transport options:	**None**
Alternative route:	**To Gruben via the Forcletta (see brief note below)**

This undemanding day's walk leads out of French-speaking Valais and into German-speaking Wallis; the same canton but linguistically a world apart from that through which you've been walking since crossing the Col de Balme.

And it's not just the language that changes either, for a different set of landscapes are in view – quite unlike anything yet seen on the walk. On leaving Hotel Weisshorn the way leads through a curiously contorted country en route to the Meidpass (or Meiden Pass as it is also known), while the way down to the Turtmanntal is a descent into the past. The Turtmanntal seems not to belong to the present century – there is a motor road, it is true, and both the Hotel Schwarzhorn and Restaurant Waldesruh have all modern amenities, yet a profound sense of peace prevails and the valley appears to remain untouched by pressures from the 'outside world'. It is only occupied for part of the year.

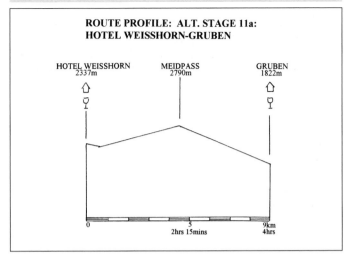

ROUTE PROFILE: ALT. STAGE 11a:
HOTEL WEISSHORN-GRUBEN

HOTEL WEISSHORN
2337m

MEIDPASS
2790m

GRUBEN
1822m

0   5   9km
2hrs 15mins   4hrs

It must be said that while the Meidpass route is both direct and inter-esting, it does not have the scenic qualities of the Forcletta alternative. This latter crossing (2874m) has already been described from Zinal (Stage 11), but it would be perfectly feasible to use that pass when starting from Hotel Weisshorn. Arguably it gives a better day's walk than the Meidpass route without adding greatly to the time taken on that crossing, and is therefore outlined below as an option.

First the route via the Forcletta:
This is signed above Hotel Weisshorn. A path takes you through the hanging valley on the east side of the Pointes de Nava which run in a line south of the hotel. At the head of this little hanging valley above the pastures of Tsa du Touno you cross a 2621m saddle and descend on the south side to a track/farm road. Bear left and shortly come to the long cowsheds at the alp of **TSAHALET** (2523m) where you join the main route described as Stage 11 above.

The direct route to Gruben via the Meidpass is as follows:
Above Hotel Weisshorn follow the track as it curves round to the right, in effect retracing the very last stage of yesterday's approach. This delivers you to a view overlooking a geologically interesting basin

opposite the 'island peak' of Le Touno (3018m). Continue beyond the initial signpost to a second where the route to Meidpass is first given. Wander down a track that winds leftwards through a confused, chaotic patch of country scoured out by a glacial system whose icy remnants disappeared long ago. The track takes you below Le Touno, crosses a stream, then strikes northward until, about 30 minutes from Hotel Weisshorn, you come to a collection of old white stone buildings and a junction of tracks.

Go past the farm buildings for a few paces, then bear right on a vague signposted path towards the Meiden Pass, crossing a rough pastureland. As you gain height so the way becomes more distinct on a partial track. This leads to an isolated alp hut about 10 minutes above the previous alp buildings. The hut stands in a walled enclosure and you must pass round its left-hand side to a signpost and a narrow path continuing upvalley over more pastureland. Ahead a jagged ridge (Meidzand) creates an intriguing skyline.

The path winds steadily uphill veering slightly left, and then follows beside a small stream for a short distance to another footpath junction. (The right-hand trail goes to a little tarn, Lac de Combavert 2442m.) Continue straight ahead; the way is marked with MP painted in blue lettering on a rock.

This brings you into a wild upper mountain basin with crags and screes above. The path adopts a comfortable gradient and zig-zags to the ridge, gaining **MEIDPASS** (2790m 2 hours 15 mins) with its starkly contrasting views. Just before reaching the pass you gaze back to the distant Mont Blanc de Cheilon, Grand Combin and even Mont Blanc itself. But now to the south-east one looks over another somewhat desolate, stony wasteland, to more big snow and ice peaks. The Brunegghorn (3833m) and Weisshorn once again look impressive.

The Meidpass is a narrow, stony saddle slung between upstanding rotten-looking blocks: Corne du Boeuf, or Meidspitz, to the north, Pigne de Combavert to the south. The way down to the Turtmanntal is an easy zig-zag route that soon strikes leftwards to the edge of the Meidsee tarn (2661m). You then descend into a modest pastureland on a clear path with the Meidhorn (2875m) guarding it on the right.

There was no wind, no breeze, no sound of streams or falling stones, nor of marmot, sheep or cowbell. We were both so struck by the overpowering sense of peace and stillness that we stopped for a minute and listened. And it was true. It was as though even the Earth itself had ceased to spin; as though all and everything had momentarily been frozen in time. There were no sounds. Before I had always believed that so long as there was life there could be no such thing as silence – there would be some semblance of sound, if only the hum of distance. But this was the nearest I had ever come to total soundlessness. We'd entered a zone of silence.

The path leads to an alp hamlet at 2334m (**OBER STAFEL** – the 'upper alp'), beyond which you come to a lip of hillside and drop steeply to the lower alp (**MITTEL STAFEL**) with a grand view upvalley to the Turtmann glacier, and off to the left to the glaciers of Wildstrubel and Balmhorn in the Bernese Alps, and to the cone of the lovely Bietschhorn[(1)] (3934m) which rises above the Lötschental on the far side of the unseen Rhône valley.

Below Mittel Stafel you enter a forest of stone pine and larch and descend without too much knee-jarring to the valley floor. Cross the Turtmänna stream by a bridge and walk up the opposite slope to reach the small village of **GRUBEN**.

GRUBEN (MEIDEN) (1822m 4 hours) *Accommodation, refreshments, shop.*

Hotel Schwarzhorn (beds & matratzenlager/dortoir) ☎ *(027) 932 14 14 – open June to October; Restaurant Waldesruh (5 minutes down-valley; matratzenlager)* ☎ *(027) 932 13 97 – open mid-June to mid-September.*

Places or Features of Interest Along the Way:

1: THE BIETSCHHORN: This impressive and very difficult peak ("whose attractions are so overwhelming that it cannot escape perpetual attraction" – according to R L G Irving) is seen to the north in the line of the Bernese Alps. An isolated mountain of 3934 metres, it stands high above the tranquil Lötschental which it dominates by its powerful presence, and was first climbed by Leslie Stephen and his guides on 13 August 1859.

Distance:	**16 kilometres**
Time:	**7½ hours**
Start altitude:	**1822m**
High point:	**Augstbordpass 2894m**
Height gain:	**1072m**
Height loss:	**1767m**
Map:	**L.S. 5006 Matterhorn–Mischabel 1:50,000**
	or L.S. 274T Visp 1:50,000
Accommodation:	**Jungen (5½ hours) – *matratzenlager***
	St Niklaus – hotels, pensions
Transport option:	**Cable-car (Jungen–St Niklaus)**

This stage is one of the finest of them all and a walk to stand comparison with almost any other day's outing in the Pennine Alps. It has so many contrasts, so many features that capture one's attention. It has history too, for the Augstbordpass which links the Turtmanntal with the Mattertal was used from the Middle Ages onward as an important trading route between the Rhône valley and Italy; a route that originally continued from St Niklaus to Zermatt and over the glacial Theodule Pass beside the Matterhorn.

Crossing the final pass on the Chamonix to Zermatt route is a highlight in every sense of the word. Never as demanding as the total height gain and loss might suggest, it leads through spacious woodland, over high pastures and into a stony wilderness, but then opens to some of the loveliest views in all Switzerland. The Matterhorn does not feature in these views, however, but remains hidden until you are committed to the Europaweg on the far side of the Mattertal. But other high peaks – most notably the Dom (the highest peak entirely within Swiss territory) – add much to the scene, while the Mattertal itself appears as an incredibly deep trench of greenery walled by grey rock and forest another world away.

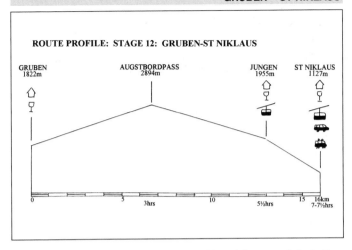

ROUTE PROFILE: STAGE 12: GRUBEN-ST NIKLAUS

GRUBEN
1822m

AUGSTBORDPASS
2894m

JUNGEN
1955m

ST NIKLAUS
1127m

0   5   3hrs   10   5½hrs   15   16km
7-7½hrs

Then comes the descent into that world, and this too is full of pleasures and the odd surprise; none greater or more beautiful than the discovery of the little hamlet of Jungen clinging to the desperately steep mountain slopes high above St Niklaus. Not an unreal tourist haunt, this is a living, working, daily active alp hamlet, and one of the last such remote farming communities to be met on the Walker's Haute Route.

From Jungen the path plunges once again into forest, dropping into the shadowed depths of the Mattertal past a series of tiny white shrines as views of the valley are rearranged with almost every step.

The way to the Augstbordpass begins on the south side of Hotel Schwarzhorn where a grassy trail heads up the slope towards sparse woods of larch and pine. It's a generous path with long weaving zigzags on which you gain height without too much effort.

In a little under an hour you will arrive at a four-way path junction (**GRÜOBUALP** 2151m 50 mins). Ignore alternatives and continue uphill (the right-hand option goes to the Turtmann Hut). Emerging from the woods pass above a lone hut and, about 15 minutes from the Grüobualp junction, come onto a dirt road which crosses the hillside towards an avalanche defence system. Bear right along it, and two minutes later cut up to the left on a continuing footpath rising up the

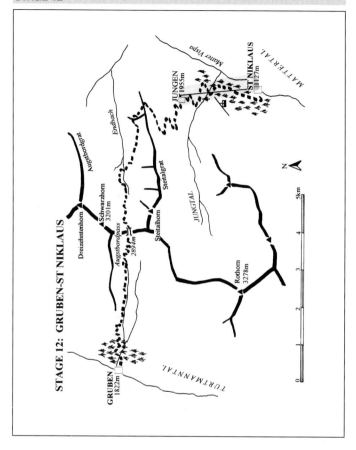

STAGE 12: GRUBEN-ST NIKLAUS

hillside. This winds up to an open shelf occupied by the two alp build-ings of **OBER GRÜOBU STAFEL** (2369m) with wide views across the valley to the Meidpass.

The path continues, passing to the right of the huts and heading uphill to the left of a stream in the hanging valley of Grüobtälli. Still without any unduly steep sections you rise to a lumpy inner region with screes lining the southern wall of peaks, and grassy hummocks

*On the approach to the Augstbordpass,
with Meidpass in the background*

elsewhere littered with grey-green lichened rocks. As with the basin below the Meidpass, this area too is a place where few sounds intrude on a windless day.

After about 2½ hours the trail steepens as you rise over a rocky step, then descend slightly to skirt a small pond before curving left and rising again, this time at a steady incline on the final stretch to the **AUGSTBORDPASS** (2894m 3 hours).

The pass overlooks a wild and rock-strewn wilderness, a landscape of austere beauty. Ahead in the distance rises the pointed, glacier-draped Fletschhorn[1] (3919m) above the vague hint of the Saastal, while in the middle distance northern outliers of the great Mischabel[2] wall, with Balfrin and Ulrichshorn above the Ried glacier, spread in a lavish show of grandeur.

Note: Given sufficient time, plus energy and inclination, the Schwarzhorn to the north of the pass would be worth a visit (1 hour from the pass). The panorama it affords is on a grand scale, with a reputation as one of the great viewpoints of the Alps. It is "one of surpassing magnificence": to the north a memorable spread of the Bernese Alps, including Finsteraarhorn and Doldenhorn; to the south the view takes in Monte Rosa, Liskamm, Weisshorn and Dent Blanche; and to the east the Ticino Alps blaze a blue horizon, while nearer to hand rise the Mischabel chain, Weissmies, Fletschhorn and Monte Leone.

A clear path drops in zig-zags to a stony bowl on the eastern side; the cirque that cups the Inners Tälli. Steeply at first, the way eases lower down and 25 minutes from the pass squeezes through a rocky cleft, emerging to scant grass littered with rocks. About 10 minutes later you come to a junction of paths, taking the right-hand option (signed to Jungen and St Niklaus) that slopes down and then veers over to the right-hand side of the valley after crossing the Emdbach stream.

The route now embarks on a gently rising traverse of the southern flank of the valley, heading east across a slope of boulders and rocks. But it's a well-made path and it brings you to a shoulder at 2488 metres where you gain a first sighting of the deep cut of the Mattertal.[3] Off to the left can be seen the Grosser Aletschgletscher.[4]

Continuing round the mountainside the path narrows and is exposed in places (care required). It climbs one or two rock steps then turns a spur (**TWÄRA** c2500m 4½ hours), and there before you is one of those rare sights that is so overwhelmingly powerful that all else is forgotten.

Across the gulf of the Mattertal soar Nadelhorn, Lenzspitze and Dom[5] with the Ried glacier pouring into the shoe-horn trough it has carved above Grächen's green terrace. It is a stunning vision, full of drama and grace of form, a perfect symbol of mountain architecture. (Ruskin would have loved it.) Then, right at the head of the Mattertal, Liskamm, Castor and Pollux and the long white block of the Breithorn, with the smaller pyramid of the Klein Matterhorn next to it. (The Matterhorn itself remains shyly hidden behind the black outline of the Mettelhorn.)

A few more paces and, most stunning of all, the Weisshorn yet again announces its domineering presence above and behind the Brunegghorn that rises in one immense shaft nearly two and a half thousand metres out of the valley.

This spur of mountainside, three hours above the valley, is surely the crowning glory of the Walker's Haute Route, a route that presents one visual gem after another from start to finish. (It's not over yet for there's more to come.) At least, that's how it seemed to us, for we found ourselves rooted to the spot, spellbound by the

Jungen, overlooked by the Dom from the far side of the Mattertal

panorama, perched on a sun-warmed slab of rock with more than a glimpse of heaven all around.

Now the path becomes a paved mule-track, but then narrows again as the descent proper begins, winding down in long undemanding loops. When you reach a junction of paths with a seat and a signpost (**UNTERE LÄGER** 2255m), bear right on a path marked Jungen Rundweg.

This slopes down towards the Jungtal (a hanging valley draining from the south-west), goes through a stone wall and then cuts back to the left to follow the wall for some distance before swinging to the right among trees, and then twisting down to the picturesque hamlet of **JUNGEN** (1955m 5½ hours *accommodation, refreshments, cable-car to St Niklaus*). This is a delightful collection of old timber chalets and haybarns, with a white painted chapel and nearby restaurant, the Junger-Stübli, perched high above the valley. (*Note:* The L.S. map names this hamlet Jungu.)

As soon as we saw the hamlet from the path way above it, we knew instinctively that it would offer something special, and it did. Coming down to Jungen reinforced that initial instinct. First there was the visual dimension – a quintessential alp hamlet of almost black timbers with a long, dramatic view to the head of the valley.

*The valley lay 900 metres below; the Dom (4545m) soared up to
full height opposite, a white crust above the rocky Grubenhorn,
with the Ried glacier peeling through its funnel; Brunegghorn and
Weisshorn above to the right dazzled in the afternoon sunlight.
We wandered between the buildings and, just below the chapel,
saw a restaurant, the Junger-Stübli, and couldn't resist stopping
there for a drink with that view before us. Our original plan had
been to continue down to St Niklaus, but when we realized there
was a bed to be had here, our plan changed instantly. St Niklaus
could wait until tomorrow. That evening we studied the mountains
through binoculars, noting the light of the Bordier Hut opposite
below the Balfrin, and another at the head of the valley where a
glow-worm sized train moved slowly against the black mountain
shapes towards the Gornergrat – a world remote from ours. Jungen
was full of magic and we spent a memorable night there, enjoying
first-class hospitality (that has been repeated on every return since)
in a setting that is nothing short of pure enchantment.*

A limited amount of accommodation is available here: one small
matratzenlager (dormitory) with 6 bunks and simple self-catering facilities (wood-burning stove) in a neighbouring chalet. Meals available at
the Junger-Stübli. Open June–October. Reservations to: Fam. Gruber,
Junger-Stübli, Jungen, 3924 St Niklaus ☎ (027) 956 21 01.

The path through Jungen leads to the chapel (if you prefer to
descend by cable-car turn left at an obvious junction in the middle of
the hamlet on a path that goes directly to the cableway station). From
the chapel descend steeply below the restaurant and wind in zig-zags
into forest. Beside the forest path you will pass a whole series of small
white shrines (Stations of the Cross) most of which have been dedicated by Mattertal families.

About 35 minutes below Jungen there's a footpath junction where
you continue straight ahead – the alternative trail cuts sharply back to
the left. Cross a rocky cleft on a footbridge over the Jungbach stream,
beyond which the gradient is less severe. The way winds on, still
through forest as it works round the lower hillside, then between small
parcels of meadowland to reach the railway station at **ST NIKLAUS**.[6]

ST NIKLAUS (1127m 7–7½ hours) *Accommodation, refreshments,
shops, banks, PTT, railway (to Zermatt and Visp), cable-car (to*

Jungen), bus to Grächen and Gasenried. Verkehrsbüro (tourist office), 3924 St Niklaus ☎ (027) 956 16 15.

Lower priced accommodation: Hotel La Réserve ☎ (027) 955 22 55; Pension Walliserkeller ☎ (027) 956 11 60; Pension Edelweiss ☎ (027) 956 26 16.

Note: Before deciding on overnight accommodation here consider your onward plan. Should you decide to opt for the high route to Zermatt via the Europaweg (Stages 13 & 14) you may choose to take the BVZ bus to Gasenried (saving an uphill walk of 1½–2 hours) in order to tackle the first stage of the Europaweg tomorrow. In this case the bus leaves from just outside St Niklaus railway station. (For accommodation in Gasenried refer to Stage 12a below.) However, should your plan be to walk the original valley route to Zermatt, your best bet is to overnight here in St Niklaus.

Places or Features of Interest Along the Way:

1: FLETSCHHORN: Rising high above the village of Saas Balen in the Saastal the Fletschhorn (3993m) is a mountain of some complexity and one which, though little known outside climbing circles, commands a certain respect. Its twisted ridges ensure that every view of it is different. Glaciers sweep down on each side between extended rocky spurs. Immediately to the south is the Lagginhorn with the Boshorn to the north. The Fletschhorn received its first ascent in 1854.

2: MISCHABEL: The name given to that huge wall of peaks that forms the western section of Saas Fee's noted amphitheatre and makes an effective divide between the Saastal and the Mattertal, the Mischabel wall consists of Täschhorn, Dom and Lenzspitze, with a spur going north-west to include the Nadelhorn. It's a consistently high wall whose crest nowhere falls below 4000 metres. A bivouac hut stands on the Mischabeljoch at the southern end, while the Mischabel huts (there are two) are perched on a rib of rock between the Hohbalm and smaller Fall glaciers. The western flanks are served by the Täsch, Kin, Dom and Bordier huts. Only the northern outliers of the Mischabel group are seen at first from the Augstbordpass.

3: MATTERTAL: The Vispertal strikes south from the Rhône valley for seven kilometres to Stalden, where it forks. To the south-east lies the

Saastal, cut by the Saaservispa river, while south-westward runs the Mattertal, the valley of the Mattervispa river. At its head lies Zermatt with the Matterhorn towering over it. The Mattertal is a narrow, deeply-cut valley, flanked by the highest peaks in Switzerland. The eastern wall is that of the Mischabelhörner (see above), the western wall contains such magnificent peaks as Zinalrothorn, Schalihorn, Weisshorn, Bishorn and Brunegghorn, while the valley is blocked in the south by the glacier-hung mountains that run westward from Monte Rosa – Liskamm, Castor, Pollux, Breithorn and Matterhorn.

4: GROSSER ALETSCHGLETSCHER: Seen to the north as a great ice river on the far side of the Rhône valley, the Grosser Aletschgletscher is the longest glacier in the Alps. It flows for some 25 kilometres, draining such Oberland peaks as Mittaghorn, Gletscherhorn, Jungfrau, Mönch and Fiescherhorn. Some very fine walks, accessible from Riederalp, Bettmeralp or Kühboden, may be had on footpaths that run alongside the lower reaches of this glacier.

5: DOM: At 4545 metres the Dom is the highest individual mountain in Switzerland, since the Dufourspitze on Monte Rosa (4634m) is shared with Italy. The summit tops the Mischabel wall. From it the Festi glacier flows steeply westward, while the Hohberggletscher falls to the north-west and is fed by the neighbouring Lenzspitze and Nadelhorn. The normal ascent route from the Dom Hut follows the right bank of the Festigletscher, crosses the Festijoch and then makes a broad sweep up the head of the Hohberggletscher towards the summit. The Dom was first climbed in 1858, and received an early ski ascent (by Arnold Lunn and Joseph Knubel) in 1917.

6: ST NIKLAUS: This is the main village of the valley, formerly known as Gassen. St Niklaus has a 17th-century church with an onion-domed spire similar to many seen in the Tyrol. Home to a number of well-known guiding families of the Golden Age and post-Golden Age of Mountaineering, including the Knubels and Pollingers, today St Niklaus is busy with through-traffic heading upvalley to Zermatt.

Distance:	**4 kilometres**
Time:	**1½–2 hours**
Start altitude:	**1127m**
High point:	**Gasenried 1659m**
Height gain:	**532m**
Map:	**L.S. 5006 Matterhorn–Mischabel 1:50,000**
	or L.S. 274T Visp 1:50,000
Accommodation:	**Gasenried – hotel**
Transport option:	**BVZ bus (St Niklaus–Gasenried)**
Alternative routes:	**St Niklaus to Grächen (see below)**
	St Niklaus to Zermatt via the Mattertal –
	see Alternative Stage 13

This very short walk is an important linking stage which brings the Haute Route trekker to the start of the two-day Europaweg leading to Zermatt. As mentioned at the end of the previous stage, an alternative option would be to take the BVZ bus from St Niklaus to Gasenried – either on arrival at St Niklaus, or early next morning to enable you to set off fresh for the Europa Hut. Since the first stage of the Europaweg leading to the Europa Hut is quite demanding, it would not be advisable to add this (admittedly short) walk to the beginning. Better to have a comfortable night in Gasenried before setting out. There are some pleasant, scenic local walks above the village to help fill the day.

Since there's only one hotel in Gasenried (and this modestly-priced) it is advisable to telephone ahead to ensure there are beds available. Should the hotel be fully booked an alternative suggestion is to walk (or bus) to Grächen where there's plenty of accommodation. An outline of the route to Grächen is given below, and it's an easy 30 minute walk from there to Gasenried for the continuing Europaweg.

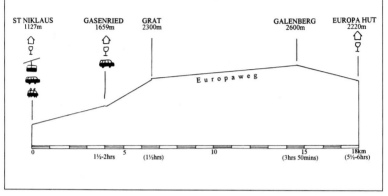

ROUTE PROFILE: STAGE 12a: ST NIKLAUS-GASENRIED
STAGE 13: GASENRIED-EUROPA HUT

From the village square below St Niklaus railway station walk down an alley to the main road and cross directly ahead into Eyeweg. This leads to a new bridge over the Mattervispa river which you cross and turn left. After passing a number of houses come to a major road. Over this walk along a minor road rising among more houses. It curves to the right and reaches a staggered crossroads. Once again cross over and continue ahead. When the road ends on the edge of woodland a footpath takes the onward route over a stream, then climbs among trees. On emerging from the woods this path makes a rising traverse of the steeply sloping hillside overlooking the northern outskirts of St Niklaus.

About 20 minutes above St Niklaus you come to a collection of old timber chalets (**WICHUL** 1195m) where you bear right onto a narrow road. This curves sharply to the right about 50 metres later.

Note: The route to Grächen slants left, rising among pinewoods, crosses and recrosses the road on the way to **RITTINEN** (1455m 1 hour 15 mins), then via **NIEDER-GRÄCHEN** 15 minutes later, where a footpath climbs among chalets and haybarns to reach the attractive resort of **GRÄCHEN**[1] (1615m 2 hours).

GRÄCHEN: *Accommodation, restaurants, shops, banks, PTT, bus (St Niklaus–Grächen). Tourismusbüro (tourist office), Dorfplatz, 3925 Grächen ☎ (027) 956 27 27.*

Lower priced accommodation: Alpha (b&b rates plus self-catering facilities) ☎ (027) 956 13 01; Zum See ☎ (027) 956 24 24; Hotel Sonne ☎ (027) 956 11 07.

The onward route to Gasenried begins by the parish church on Dorfplatz and is well-signed. It is part of the Europaweg, and takes an easy 30 minutes to join Stage 13.

From Wichul to Gasenried:
Keep to the road for a few more paces, then go sharply left then right on a narrow footpath climbing along the edge of a meadow to emerge onto the St Niklaus–Grächen road. Turn left, and almost immediately break to the right on the continuing footpath rising among woods of larch and pine.

Climbing in fairly steep zig-zags through forest the way emerges onto the road again. Bear right and turn the hairpin bend from which you gain a tremendous view upvalley. About 100 metres after the hairpin cut back to the right on a track rising among trees. When it forks soon after by a timber building take the upper route. This winds uphill, and on reaching a four-way path junction (1 hour from St Niklaus) you continue ahead. The next junction is met by a shrine and a crucifix where you bear right to make a final climb to Gasenried, soon passing between vegetable plots with the village seen above.

The lower part of the village is reached in about 1 hour 20 minutes, and from here you gain views north to the Bernese Alps, with the pointed Bietschhorn prominent in that view. Follow a narrow road which rises steeply to the main part of **GASENRIED**[2] where the Ried glacier is seen at the head of a hanging valley behind the village. The only hotel, the Alpenrösli, is situated in the square near the church.

GASENRIED (1659m 1 hour 40 mins) *Accommodation, restaurants, shop, PTT, BVZ bus (St Niklaus–Gasenried). Tourismusbüro, Dorfplatz, 3925 Grächen ☎ (027) 956 27 27.*

Hotel Alpenrösli, Gasenried/Grächen, 3924 St Niklaus ☎ (027) 956 22 42 Fax: (027) 956 30 25 – 28 beds; open June–October.

The Ried glacier above Gasenried

Places or Features of Interest Along the Way:

1: GRÄCHEN: Sprawling along a sun-trap of terraced hillside on the east side of the Mattertal, about 500 metres above St Niklaus, this attractive resort attracts visitors in winter and summer. By judicious use of the Seetalhorn and Hannigalp cableways some tremendous view-points are easily accessible, but even without this mechanical aid there are numerous footpaths that give scenically rewarding walks. There are two classic long walks from here. The first is the Balfrin Höhenweg (or Höhenweg Saas Fee as it's also known) which makes a challenging high-level route to Saas Fee by a series of former shepherds' paths, and was opened in 1954. This takes 7–7½ hours to complete. The other long route is the 31 kilometre Europaweg (opened July 1997) between Grächen and Zermatt, which now forms the last two stages of the Chamonix to Zermatt Walker's Haute Route. With plenty of accommo-dation choices, Grächen makes a good base for a walking holiday.

2: GASENRIED: This low-key neighbour of Grächen's is dug into the steep hillside a little further south. The village stands on two levels and consists of a number of typical Valaisian chalets and granaries, while just above it footpaths cut through steep pastures and forests to extend the views. The valley of the Riedbach torrent lies behind Gasenried, with the Ried glacier hanging in its upper reaches. As a holiday base, Gasenried would suit walkers disinterested in 'night life'. It's a quiet place with lots of opportunities for walkers.

Distance:	**18 kilometres**
Time:	**5½ hours**
Start altitude:	**1127m**
High point:	**Zermatt 1606m**
Height gain:	**479m**
Maps:	**L.S. 5006 Matterhorn–Mischabel 1:50,000 or L.S. 274T Visp & 284T Mischabel 1:50,000**
Accommodation:	**Mattsand (40 mins) – hotel**
	Herbriggen (1 hour 10 mins) – hotel
	Randa (2½ hours) – hotel, pension, camping
	Täsch (3½ hours) – hotels, camping
	Zermatt – hotels, youth hostel, camping
Transport option:	**Train (St Niklaus–Zermatt)**
Alternative route:	**St Niklaus to Gasenried, then along Europaweg (2 days) to Zermatt – see Stages 12a & 13/14**

Until the Europaweg was created (see Stages 13 & 14) this was taken as the final stage of the long walk from Chamonix to Zermatt, and although it has been eclipsed by that high and challenging trail, this valley walk will still be the preferred choice for those with limited time or as a bad-weather alternative. It is something of a tease, for naturally the Matterhorn is what you hope to see, but it remains hidden until the very end.

The walk, it must be said, is by no means the most scenic of the Haute Route for it never strays far from road or railway, and views are necessarily limited by the steep valley walls. However, it is not as uninteresting as you might fear, for there are hamlets and villages along the

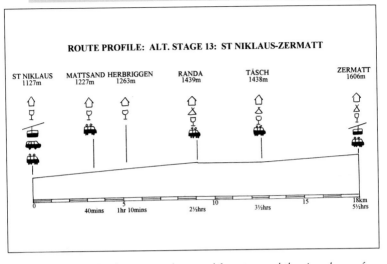

ROUTE PROFILE: ALT. STAGE 13: ST NIKLAUS-ZERMATT

way, ancient haybarns, meadows and forests – and the river, born of glaciers and great snowfields, for company along much of the route.

Cross the village square below St Niklaus railway station and bear right, then left down a narrow street to the main road. Turn right and walk upvalley almost to the outskirts of the village (about 400 metres), where the road curves left to cross a bridge over the river. Here you must break to the right on a small side road between chalets.

The way now follows what is apparently the 'old' road through the valley, bringing you alongside the Brig–Visp–Zermatt (BVZ) railway line and passing some typical old Valaisian houses, as well as more modern buildings based on traditional architectural styles. (There's plenty of accommodation to be had along this stretch of road.) Pass beneath the railway and before long you arrive in **MATTSAND** (1227m 40 mins *accommodation at Hotel Mattsand* ☎ *(027) 956 16 80).*

Still on the old road cross back over the railway line to skirt a large settlement reservoir, and when the tarmac road bears left round the southern end, go directly ahead on a continuing track.

About one hour from St Niklaus the track brings you to a junction by a collection of haybarns. Continue upvalley along the right-hand side of the Mattervispa river between more pastures, then down to a

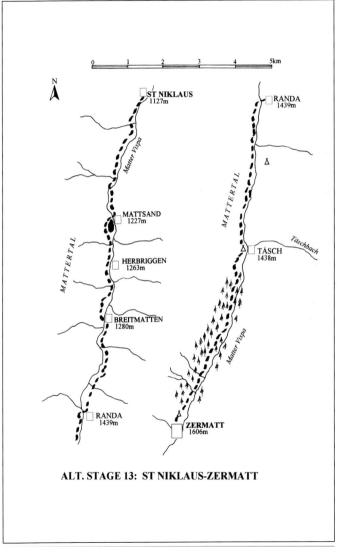

ALT. STAGE 13: ST NIKLAUS-ZERMATT

footbridge that leads over the river to **HERBRIGGEN** (1262m 1 hour 10 mins, *accommodation at Hotel Bergfreund* ☎ *(027) 956 19 69*). Do not cross over, but remain on the west side of the river on a foot-path signed to Randa, Täsch and Zermatt.

The path accompanies the Mattervispa for a while, then climbs a little beyond a barn and reaches a junction of trails where you bear left. Wind uphill among trees on a very pleasant narrow path before dropping again to the river bank (**ROSSWANG**) and across a footbridge to the main valley road on the edge of **BREITMATTEN** (1280m). Thanks to a massive rockfall[1] it is now necessary to walk up the road for about 30 minutes. Keep on the left side of the road to face oncoming traffic, and use the grass verge where possible. In half an hour or so of road walking you will come to the outskirts of Randa.[2] Although the route does not enter the village proper, a short diversion is worth taking should you need refreshment. In addition to the accommodation facil-ities listed below, Randa has restaurants, shops and tourist information ☎ *(027) 967 16 77*.

RANDA (1439m 2½ hours *accommodation: Pension Sporting* ☎ *(027) 967 67 62; Hotel Dom* ☎ *(027) 967 35 56; camping*).

Shortly before reaching the railway station leave the main road, go down to the right on a feeder road and cross the river just beyond a gravel works. Once over the bridge turn left on a riverside path – attrac-tive, mostly level and easy walking. This will take you all the way to Täsch[3] in about an hour, and Zermatt in approximately three hours.

TÄSCH (1438m 3½ hours *Hotel Elite* ☎ *(027) 967 12 26; Hotel City* ☎ *(027) 967 36 06; camping*). There are other hotels, as well as restaurants, shops, bank, PTT and tourist information ☎ *(027) 967 16 89*. Most of these are clustered near the railway station.

Again, as with Randa, it is not necessary to cross into Täsch unless you need any of its facilities. Instead, remain on the west bank of the river and pass alongside the campsite. As far as Täsch the footpath was gentle and undemanding, but now the trail begins to climb among woods, dodging to and fro near the railway. It's a clear and well-trodden path that leads directly to Zermatt.[4]

Reluctant to finish the walk we sat on a bench on the outskirts of Zermatt. Since first light we'd had rain and knee-high clouds which somehow helped counter-balance all the fine-weather days. If views were to be denied us, this was definitely the day for it. Of course, that meant no Matterhorn, but what we had experienced in the previous two weeks more than made up for that loss. At Täsch the rain had stopped, but low clouds still obscured every view. Seated on the damp bench outside Zermatt we reviewed the walk as a whole, and concluded that it had been one of the most beautiful either of us had ever undertaken. (Between us we had more than fifty years of mountain experience.) Without doubt we'd be back to walk it again (as we have, several times). But for now we were in no hurry for it to be over. For all its undeniable attractions and for all its being the culmination of the walk that had begun on a sunny afternoon in Chamonix, Zermatt was not going to be another of those quiet, unassuming hamlets that had added so much to the route. We were about to face the crowds – and that would be a culture shock. So we sat among the clouds and put off the final ten-minute stroll into town. And we'd still be sitting there now had the rain not started once more.

(PS: Next day we were blessed with blue skies and sunshine, and so wandered upvalley with eyes transfixed by the sight of that great pyramid of rock. Our pilgrimage from Chamonix to Zermatt – Mont Blanc to the Matterhorn – was complete.)

ZERMATT (1606m 5½ hours) *Accommodation, camping, restaurants, shops, banks, PTT, railway (to Visp, Brig, Geneva, etc). Tourismusbüro (tourist office), Bahnhofplatz, 3920 Zermatt* ☎ *(027) 967 01 81 E-mail: Zermatt@Wallis.ch Website: www.zermatt.ch*

For accommodation please see details listed at the end of Stage 14.

Places or Features of Interest Along the Way:

1: ROCKFALL NEAR RANDA: In April 1991 a massive rockfall reshaped the mountainside northwest of Randa when a vast section of the Langenflueberg collapsed into the valley, demolishing the railway, blocking the river and cutting off the upper Mattertal for several days. Hundreds of large boulders still litter the valley where they came to rest in the meadows – close to chalets and haybarns – just below Randa.

2: RANDA: Situated in the valley midway between the Weisshorn and the Dom, this attractive village is developing into a low-key alternative to Zermatt. It stands above the main Mattertal road and railway, and so is relieved of through-traffic pressure. From the village a steep path climbs to the Europa Hut in 2¼ hours (see Stage 13) and the higher Dom Hut in 4 hours. On the other side of the valley a 4¼ hour walk leads to the Weisshorn Hut. Apart from these lofty destinations, there are other good walks to be tackled from this valley base. The campsite, just to the south of Randa, has excellent facilities and views of the Zinalrothorn.

3: TÄSCH: Noted for the monstrous car parks which fill the meadows to the north of the railway station, Täsch is where the great majority of motoring visitors to Zermatt leave their vehicles before catching the train for the final leg of the journey upvalley. (Motor vehicles are banned from Zermatt.) The village that most people see is so dominated by this traffic that it has little identity of its own – almost everything here leans towards Zermatt. However, the original village stands aloof from all this on the west side of the valley, and is much more attractive and typically Valaisian in its architecture. Behind it a steeply twisting service road climbs the hillside and enters the lovely, unspoilt Täschbach glen in which lies the hamlet of Täschalp, and above which stands the Täsch Hut. There are some peaceful and scenic walks to be had up there, including sections of the Europaweg adopted by Stage 14.

4: ZERMATT: As one of the great Alpine resorts Zermatt has no real closed season – it's busy throughout the year; if not with skiers, walkers or climbers, then with the crowds of general tourists who flock there either to pay homage to the Matterhorn or to add the town to the tick-list of European hot-spots. Zermatt has something for everyone, and it's impossible to be bored there. If you don't like the crowds, there are paths that lead to magnificent viewpoints where even in the height of summer you can experience true solitude, and no shortage of other trails that, while not being empty, are well worth taking for their variety and extravagent panoramas. (See Appendix A for a sample.) If you're stuck in town on a wet day, why not visit the interesting Alpine Museum near the post office?

STAGE 13:

GASENRIED – EUROPA HUT

Distance:	14 kilometres
Time:	5½–6 hours
Start altitude:	1659m
High point:	North of Galenberg 2690m
Height gain:	1031m
Height loss:	470m
Maps:	L.S. 5006 Matterhorn–Mischabel 1:50,000 or L.S. 274T Visp & 284T Mischabel 1:50,000
Accommodation:	Europa Hut – mountain refuge
Transport option:	None
Alternative route:	St Niklaus to Zermatt via the Mattertal – see Alternative Stage 13

In the first two editions of this guide the final stage of the Walker's Haute Route was necessarily confined to the valley bed where a series a footpaths led from one village to the next between St Niklaus and Zermatt (now described as Alternative Stage 13). But in the summer of 1997 the so-called Europaweg, a 31 kilometre high route between Grächen and Zermatt, was completed, thereby enabling the Haute Route to be just that right to the end. However, it soon became apparent that the distance between possible lodgings along the Europaweg was too great for most walkers to manage within a single day, so two years later the Randa *gemeinde* built in record-time the splendid Europa Hut almost exactly halfway along the trail. So the finalé of the Walker's Haute Route from Chamonix to Zermatt is now a two-day trek along this magnificent path.

The Europaweg is a challenging route which climbs high above the Mattertal – as much as 1400 metres above the valley in some places –

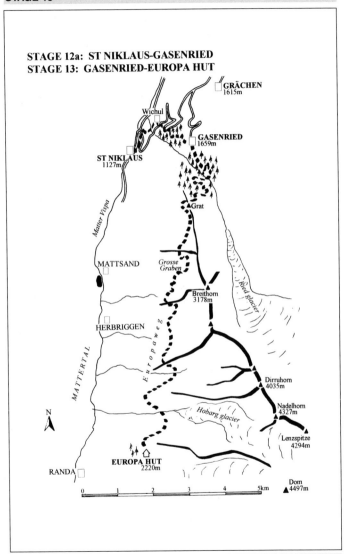

STAGE 12a: ST NIKLAUS-GASENRIED
STAGE 13: GASENRIED-EUROPA HUT

GRÄCHEN
1615m

Wichul

GASENRIED
1659m

ST NIKLAUS
1127m

Mauer Vispa

Grat

MATTSAND

Grosse
Graben

Ried glacier

Breithorn
3178m

HERBRIGGEN

Europaweg

Dirruhorn
4035m

MATTERTAL

Nadelhorn
4327m

Hobarg glacier

Lenzspitze
4294m

N

EUROPA HUT
2220m

RANDA

0   1   2   3   4   5km

Dom
4497m

with one tremendous viewpoint after another to make it a visual extravaganza virtually from start to finish. One of the best panoramas is enjoyed less than two hours after setting out, when the Matterhorn at last reveals itself at the head of the valley, the Bietschhorn is seen in the other direction, Dom and Ried glacier to the south-east, and Weisshorn to the south-west, plus numerous other peaks each of which would be a major attraction in any other range. Make sure you have plenty of film for your camera and make an early start so you have time to pause often along the way.

Warning: It will take a total of 11–12 hours to walk these two stages from Gasenried to Zermatt, and by far the majority of the Europaweg is as safe as can be expected of a high mountain path. However, it is necessary to point out that there are several places (the first about 2½ hours from Gasenried) that are potentially dangerous from stonefall or other objective hazards where walkers are urged to be extra vigilant and to move quickly over the danger areas – a total of about 20 minutes for the whole walk, to put it into perspective. There are countless sections safeguarded with lengths of fixed rope too, and (on Stage 14) a narrow 100 metre tunnel through a rock wall without illumination. The Europaweg, which is publicised as part of the misnamed 'Swiss Tour of Monte Rosa', has become extremely popular, especially with local Swiss walkers, but everyone who tackles it should make his or her own judgement whether the risks outlined here (and marked with warning signs on the trail itself) are worth taking. Should you think not, then follow the one-day valley route described as Alternative Stage 13.

And finally, you are strongly advised to telephone ahead to the Europa Hut to book bedspace for the night. In the high season it is likely to be very busy.

Follow the road past the church in Gasenried curving left into the Riedbach valley. On reaching a small chapel the road forks. Take the upper option which becomes a track leading into woods where the valley narrows to a gorge. In 14 minutes the way forks (left to Gletschertor, etc); continue ahead, swinging right to cross the glacial torrent on a footbridge. Just over the bridge take the upper path where it divides, and wander easily through the woods to a signed junction (20 mins from the start). Remain on the upper route, the gradient now becoming steeper.

In a little over 50 minutes the path forks once more (c1990m); the left branch goes to Alpja and the Bordier Hut, but ours veers right (signed to Galenberg and the Europa Hut). Gaining height occasional views are glimpsed through the trees to the Bietschhorn in the distance, and Gasenried below. In just over 1½ hours reach a viewpoint (**GRAT** 2300m) with a stunning panorama that concentrates on the chain of the Bernese Alps and the gleaming Grosser Aletschgletscher, while through a gap spiky peaks on the west side of the Mattertal will be recognised as being on show on the descent into the Turtmanntal from the Forcletta on Stage 11. Just above the viewpoint a large cross extends the view and makes a very fine belvedere.

The path now curves through the rocky gap to a view of the Barrhorn and Weisshorn, and five minutes later you gain another wonderful viewpoint at 2335m marked by a signpost, from where the unmistakable Matterhorn can be seen upvalley. Bear left and climb higher up the ridge guided by waymarks and cairns, to emerge onto a broad open shoulder on which there's a statue of St Bernard[1] off to the left (c2460m 2 hours). From this point the Riedgletscher is seen to good effect to the south-east – the Bordier Hut can also be seen from here on the east bank of the glacier.

The Europaweg continues to rise, crossing a rocky area to another path junction where you continue straight ahead. Here the trail has been forced across a very rough slope, and about 2½ hours from Gasenried you reach the first major area exposed to stonefall; the Grosse Graben combe. Much of this combe is in an unstable condition, and a sign warns to cross the danger area quickly. A combination of caution and speed is advised.

On the south side of the combe beneath the Breithorn (one of a number of Swiss mountains to bear this name) there are several fixed rope sections, but rounding a rocky spur at about 2690 metres (3 hours) you reach the highest part of the Europaweg and gain yet more stunning views of the Weisshorn. The way then descends a little, then zig-zags up to pass round another spur and contours to a wooden walkway followed by another fixed rope section. Just beyond this another signpost gives 35 minutes to Galenberg, and 1 hour 50 mins to the hut.

Views now include the snowy mass of the Zermatt Breithorn at the head of the valley on the border with Italy. There follows another lengthy fixed rope section, and in 3 hours 50 minutes you come to the **GALENBERG** junction (2600m) where one path descends to

Herbriggen, which lies in the valley midway between St Niklaus and Randa (a 2 hour descent). At this junction take the upper path ahead, now with a clear view across the valley to the site of a massive rockfall above Randa.[2] After rising a little the path now loops down to lose about 250 metres of height, and reaches yet another path junction (4½ hours).

The way curves into a hillside 'bay' overhung by séracs of the Hobärg glacier. There is some minor danger of falling ice, and for a short stretch there are warning signs by the path. Cross the glacial torrent on a footbridge, contour round the south side of the 'bay' and come to the Miesboden spur (2280m), another splendid viewpoint. From here the path twists down among a few larches to reach the **EUROPA HUT**, a fine timber-built refuge opened in 1999 with views directly across the valley to the Weisshorn, and upvalley to the Breithorn, Klein Matterhorn, Mettelhorn and Schalihorn.

THE EUROPA HUT (2220m 5½–6 hours) *Owned by the Randa gemeinde, open mid-June to mid-October, 42 places, full meals service* ☎ *(027) 967 82 47 Fax: (027) 967 60 74.*

Places or Features of Interest Along the Way:

1: ST BERNARD: The statue of St Bernard on the great viewpoint of the Mittelberg ridge commemorates the opening of the Europaweg in 1997. This patron saint of mountain travellers was formerly Archdeacon of Aosta, Bernard of Menthon, who had spent many years caring for travellers and pilgrims in trouble after crossing the alpine pass named after him, and who was responsible for the construction of the original hospice there. Bernard died in the 1080s and was beatified shortly after. In 1923 Pope Pius XI confirmed St Bernard as patron saint of the Alps.

2: ROCKFALL NEAR RANDA: In April 1991 a massive rockfall reshaped the mountainside northwest of Randa when a vast section of the Langenflueberg collapsed into the valley, demolishing the railway, blocking the river and cutting off the upper Mattertal for several days.

STAGE 14:

EUROPA HUT – TÄSCHALP – ZERMATT

Distance:	18 kilometres
Time:	6½–7 hours
Start altitude:	2220m
High point:	Sunnegga 2288m
Height gain:	348m
Height loss:	962m
Map:	L.S. 5006 Matterhorn–Mischabel 1:50,000 or L.S. 284T Mischabel 1:50,000
Accommodation:	Täschalp (Ottavan) (3¼ hours) – *matratzenlager*
	Zermatt – hotels, pensions, *matratzenlager*, youth hostel, camping
Transport options:	Sunnegga Express funicular (Sunnegga–Zermatt)
	Bus (Winkelmatten–Zermatt)

This final stage of the Europaweg makes a worthy conclusion to the Walker's Haute Route. Visually exciting and fairly taxing (though not quite as demanding as yesterday's walk) the route is lured on by the Matterhorn which acts as a beacon for much of the way. There's rather more height gain and loss than may be suggested by the bare statistics quoted above, although the gradients are less gruelling than on some previous stages. One may expect to see chamois and marmots along the way, but it is the constant rearrangement of views that help to make this a classic and memorable finish to the long walk.

Refreshments are to be had at Täschalp, a little over three hours' walk from the Europa Hut, and again at Tufteren nearly two hours later. Thereafter there will be several other opportunities to relax with a drink in view of lofty mountains before you enter Zermatt 'by the back door'.

Note: It may be worth keeping your headtorch accessible for the passage through a rock tunnel.

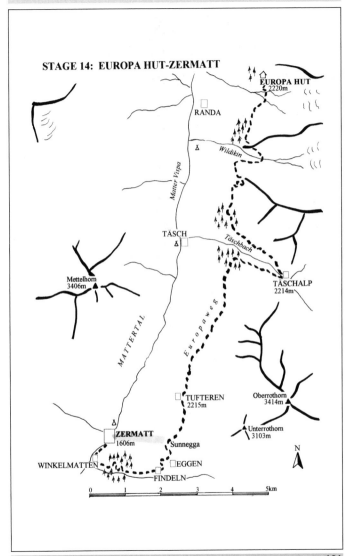

STAGE 14: EUROPA HUT-ZERMATT

EUROPA HUT
2220m

RANDA

Matter Vispa

Wildikin

TÄSCH

Täschbach

TÄSCHALP
2214m

Mettelhorn
3406m

Europaweg

MATTERTAL

TUFTEREN
2215m

Oberrothorn
3414m

Unterrothorn
3103m

ZERMATT
1606m

Sunnegga

N

WINKELMATTEN

EGGEN

FINDELN

0   1   2   3   4   5km

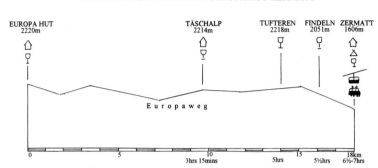

ROUTE PROFILE: STAGE 14: EUROPA HUT–ZERMATT

On leaving the Europa Hut the path slopes downhill and five minutes later comes to a junction with the Dom Hut path. Continue to descend and in another five minutes a second junction (**DOMHÜTTENWEG** 2149m) directs the Europaweg straight ahead, while the alternative path descends to Randa.

The way now slants uphill to hug a band of cliffs where you duck behind a waterfall. Soon after cross another rockfall area, beyond which you pass through sparse larchwoods and come to yet another path junction with a second descent option to Randa. On emerging from the woods the Matterhorn[1] comes into view ahead.

About 40 minutes from the hut a long uphill section of fixed ropes leads to more larchwoods and a sign to the new Kinhütte (open 2001). Our path descends a little and shortly turns a spur to enter the **WILDIKIN** combe. It is here that the path has been engineered through a tunnel about 100 metres long (as it curves inside the rockface very little light can penetrate far, so a headtorch may be useful). Out of the tunnel a steel footbridge spans the Wildibach torrent draining the Kingletscher, then the path curves round the south side of the combe and in 1½ hours turns the spur to leave it.

Now the Matterhorn, Klein Matterhorn and Breithorn provide a focus at the head of the valley. Ignoring another descent option to Randa the Europaweg makes a winding descent of the west flank of the Leiterspitzen in order to avoid a rock band and an unstable scree slope. After losing a considerable amount of height the path then tucks under an avalanche defence system (completed in 1997) with a projecting concrete lip to deflect falling stones. A series of short corrugated iron tunnels (no torch necessary) carries the route below the slope, before entering more larchwoods at the **TÄSCHGUFER** junction (1940m 2 hours 25 mins).

A path cuts off here to Täsch, while ours continues through the woods signed to Ottavan and Zermatt – watch for chamois as you wander through these woods. Rising among slopes carpeted with alpenrose and juniper the path emerges to a splendid view of the Matterhorn, then turns into the Täschbach valley, at the head of which stands the Rimpfischhorn.

Eventually come down to a service road just below **TÄSCHALP**[2] (Ottavan 2214m 3 hours 15 mins). Walk up the road and very soon you'll pass Restaurant Täschalp (*accommodation, refreshments – open June–Sept* ☎ *(027) 967 23 01*) which also advertises as the Europaweghütte.

Just beyond the restaurant leave the road for a track going ahead to a footbridge over the Täschbach stream. Cross this and turn right onto a lovely contouring path now heading north-west with a direct view of the Schalihorn and Weisshorn on the far side of the Mattertal. Ignore alternative paths and curve round the hillside spur among larchwoods, eventually joining a track at a hairpin. Follow this uphill to a footpath junction where the Europaweg bears right.

As the trail progresses high above the Mattertal so Zermatt grows in extent, with the Matterhorn growing too at the head of the valley. So come to a track at the alp hamlet of **TUFTEREN** (2215m 5 hours *refreshments*) and a choice of routes to Zermatt. One option is to follow the track that winds downhill to Zermatt in 1½ hours; a more direct route takes a signed footpath (50 mins) which begins between alp buildings, while the preferred route is described below.

Bear left along the track leading to Sunnegga. On coming to a junction take the upper of two tracks signed to Findeln and before long reach another junction just below **SUNNEGGA** (2288m 5 hours 15 mins).

Note: For a fast and easy descent to Zermatt take the so-called Alpen-Metro 'Sunnegga Express' – an underground funicular – whose station is just above you near another restaurant.

Zermatt

The 'proper way' to conclude the Haute Route follows the continuing track and subsequent footpaths (signed) down to **FINDELN** (2051m 5½ hours *refreshments*), a pretty little alp hamlet with a small white chapel and a classic view of the Matterhorn. Beyond this hamlet follow the Winkelmatten path giving good Matterhorn views almost all the way. It passes through more larchwoods descending in long loops, crosses the Gornergrat railway and enters **WINKELMATTEN** (1672m *accommodation, refreshments*), a 'suburb' of Zermatt with which it is linked by electric bus. Turn right by the church and wander down to **ZERMATT**[3] at the end of the Chamonix to Zermatt Walker's Haute Route.

ZERMATT (1606m 6½–7 hours) *Accommodation, camping, restaurants, shops, banks, PTT, railway (to Visp, Brig, Geneva, etc). Tourismusbüro (tourist office), Bahnhofplatz, 3920 Zermatt* ☎ *(027) 967 01 81   E-mail: Zermatt@Wallis.ch   Website: www.zermatt.ch*

There are more than 60 hotels listed within Zermatt itself, and many more on the outskirts. A free-phone booking facility will be found at the tourist office by the railway station.

Lower-priced accommodation: Matterhorn Hostel (matratzen-lager) on Schlumattstr ☎ (027) 968 19 19; Jugendherberge (youth hostel, in Winkelmatten) ☎ (027) 967 23 20; Naturfreundhotel ☎ (027) 967 27 88; Hotel de la Poste ☎ (027) 967 19 32.

The campsite is located just north of the railway station – functional, no frills, but well-used by walkers and climbers ☎ (027) 967 39 21.

Places or Features of Interest Along the Way:

1: THE MATTERHORN: Standing on the borders of Switzerland and Italy like some gigantic frontier post, at 4477 metres the Matterhorn is the most easily recognised of all Alpine peaks, its distinctive pyramid shape having been adopted as the very symbol of Switzerland. Not unnaturally it is the focus of attention of practically every visitor to Zermatt, and there can be few mountain activists who do not, at some time or another, feel a longing to climb it. Edward Whymper's obsession has been shared by many in the 130-odd years that have passed since his first ascent on 14 July 1865 which, with its subsequent tragedy, has passed into history as one of the best known of all mountaineering stories. Zermatt's Alpine Museum is the place to visit if you have an interest in this story.

2: TÄSCHALP: Also known as Ottavan, this hamlet lies at the junction of the Rotbach and Täschbach glens east of Täsch. There's a restaurant/*touristenlager*, an attractive little chapel, large cowsheds and a number of chalets. Upstream the Täschalpen pastures are drained by the Mellichbach stream which flows down from glaciers hanging below the Rimpfischhorn. On the hillside north of these pastures sits the Täsch Hut, with excellent views to the Schallihorn and Weisshorn, and from which a trail leads into the Rotbach glen to the north. Accessed from Täsch in the Mattertal (minibus taxis available) by a winding service road, the Täschalp has a number of charming walks.

3: ZERMATT: One of the great Alpine resorts, Zermatt's obvious success – in terms of popularity – is inextricably linked with the Matterhorn whose noble presence overshadows the town and everything to do with it. But the Matterhorn is only one of many fine mountains visible, if not from Zermatt's crowded but traffic-free streets, certainly from the surrounding slopes. In fact there are more 4000 metre summits gathered round the head of the valley than are to be found anywhere else in the Alps. It is, of course, a mountaineer's Mecca, even though mainstream activists long ago turned their backs on the area and moved to larger mountains elsewhere. The appeal of the great snow and ice peaks remains as strong as ever to middle-ability mountaineers, while walkers of all persuasions will find sufficient scope here to fill every hour of a fortnight's holiday based on the town. But apart from outdoor activity and scenic splendour, Zermatt's sense of *chic* has as much to do with the expensive boulevards of Paris, Rome or London as it has with mountains. If you have a fortune to spend on glamorous fashion and jewellery, you might as well spend it here as in a polluted European capital. Then toast your latest accessory in champagne with the Matterhorn as a backdrop. Now that's decadent!

SHOULD YOU have a day or two in hand on arrival in Zermatt and want to make the most of your time there, the handful of walks outlined below will provide some ideas. It is just a brief sample from the many to be had, but each one has its own special attributes and is highly recommended. Other ideas may be gleaned from the regional guidebook *The Valais* (published by Cicerone Press), which is readily available in the U.K. and is also usually on sale in Zermatt's main bookshop.

1: THE SCHÖNBIEL HUT: This is one of the finest of all walks in the area giving a full day's outing – there and back. The path leads upvalley to Zmutt and beyond in full view of the Matterhorn. It takes you across glacial streams and along a moraine crest to the hut which is situated on a grassy bluff southwest of Zermatt, at 2694 metres, and with superb views onto a world of ice dominated by Dent d'Hérens and the Matterhorn. (4 hours and 11 kilometres to the hut. Allow 6½ hours for the round trip.)

2: TRIFT & HÖBALMEN: The first part of this walk climbs through the confines of the Trift gorge immediately west of Zermatt, emerging to views of a glacier-hung cirque from the Victorian Hotel du Trift. From here one is faced with several choices, but for the renowned belvedere viewpoint of Höhbalmen (2665m) a path is taken which crosses the Triftbach to the south and rises over grass slopes to turn a shoulder, beyond which you come to a wonderful broad pastureland with a great sweep of mountains and glaciers in view. At a junction of paths you can either descend to Zermatt via the alp huts of Hubel and Herbrigg (a 4 hour walk), or remain high on the continuing path that eventually descends into the Arben glen to join the Schönbiel Hut path (see Note 1). Bear left and return to Zermatt via Zmutt for a 7 hour walk.

3: THE HÖRNLI HUT: Situated at 3260 metres at the foot of the steep ridge on the Matterhorn from which it takes its name, the Hörnli Hut is where most climbers spend the night before embarking on the standard route to the summit. The hut enjoys a truly dramatic position over-looking a highway of ice leading to Monte Rosa. The walk from Zermatt is an extremely steep one (4½–5 hours), although the effort can be greatly reduced by taking the cable-car to Schwarzsee and beginning the walk there (2 hours to the hut).

4: THE MONTE ROSA HUT: Here's a glacier walk with exciting views – but it should only be attempted by walkers experienced in crossing crevassed icefields! Alternatively, simply walk as far as the glacier edge, then return to Zermatt via Riffelsee and Riffelalp (6 hours in all). First take the Gornergrat railway as far as Rotenboden (try to get a seat on the right-hand side of the carriage for the best views), and on leaving the train descend a little towards the much-photographed Riffelsee, then cross a low ridge on the left. A good path cuts across the south flank of the Gornergrat ridge (*grat* actually means 'ridge') above the Gorner glacier, from which you gaze directly at that huge ice wall of Monte Rosa, Liskamm, Castor, Pollux and Breithorn which forms the Swiss–Italian border. The path leads to the glacier edge and the route across the ice is usually marked: *do not stray from the marked route for there are many crevasses; great care is needed*. All safety precautions should be taken. Once across the glacier the way scrambles up bands of rock to gain the hut in about 2½ hours. From the Monte Rosa Hut one looks along the Gorner glacier to the distant Matterhorn – a truly memorable sight. (Allow 2–2½ hours back to Rotenboden, or 5–5½ hours to walk all the way to Zermatt.)

5: FLUHALP & FOUR MOUNTAIN TARNS: For a less-demanding day than any of the above walks, ride the underground funicular to Sunnegga at 2288 metres, descend a little, then take a signed path beyond the little Leisee tarn heading roughly east to the Stellisee, and continue to the Berghütte Fluhalp (2607m) which is backed by moraines of the Findel glacier. Leaving the inn go down a track to a path serving the little Grindjisee, then continue by scenic track and footpath to the Grüensee. A short distance beyond this tarn stands the Bärghaus Grüensee near a path junction. The right-hand trail goes down to a footbridge over the Findelbach stream. Either walk down the left bank of the stream, or cross over to the lovely alp hamlet of Findeln (visited on the final stage of the Europaweg) and descend from there to Zermatt. (A 4½ hour walk.)

APPENDIX B:

Climbing from Zermatt

GIVEN TIME at the end of the Chamonix to Zermatt trek, and taking advantage of fitness, seasoned mountain walkers may be tempted to round off their trip by making the ascent of one of Zermatt's surrounding peaks. The Matterhorn is an obvious choice, but there are plenty of others. Experienced alpinists will need no advice from this book, but are directed to the Alpine Club guide to the area: *Valais East* by Lindsay Griffin. The following notes, however, may be helpful for those with experience of climbing in Britain, but whose first visit to the Alps this is.

The first thing to understand is the scale of these mountains. After two weeks of wandering across their lower ridges you will have some idea of just how big they are, but it is only by setting out to climb them that the full stature of alpine mountains can be properly appreciated. They should never be underestimated. Unless you have a member of your party with all-round experience of climbing in the Alps, and is competent to lead a climb or two from here, my advice is to leave well alone or hire a professional guide.

Zermatt has its own mountain guide's office (*Bergführerbüro*) with 50 or more official guides working from it. The office is found on the main street south of the railway station: ☎ (027) 966 24 60. Guided excursions suitable for beginners are arranged daily, weather permitting. These include a 4 hour glacier trek from the Klein Matterhorn to Trockener Steg, basic climbing instruction on the Riffelhorn, or the ascent of such 4000 metre peaks as the Allalinhorn and Weissmies.

A variety of other peaks can be offered, but it should be stressed that to employ a professional mountain guide here can be very expensive – although that expense may be justified by the knowledge that the experience of standing on top of your first alpine peak is likely to be one you'll always remember.

The cost of employing a guide for the climb itself is only part of the expense. Add to this the guide's food in a mountain hut (an overnight is usually necessary), hut fees for yourself and the guide, and hire of equipment – you'll no doubt need crampons, plus ice-axe –

which can be rented from one of the many local sports shops. (The guide provides the rope.) It is also necessary to have mountain accident and rescue insurance.

1: THE METTELHORN: At 3406 metres this modest peak is not in the same league as those mentioned below, but is a popular 'tourist' summit because of the extent and richness of its panorama. In times past an ascent of the Mettelhorn formed part of the training programme of mountaineers newly-arrived in the area, for the 1800 metre difference in height from Zermatt to summit was considered ideal for acclimatisation and testing one's fitness! Having spent two weeks walking from Chamonix you ought to be fit by now, and the 6 hour ascent by way of the Trift gorge, involving no technical difficulty, should be within the capabilities of most C–Z trekkers.

2: THE BREITHORN: Generally considered the easiest of the local 4000 metre summits (and possibly the easiest for its height in the Alps), the 4164m Breithorn is situated midway between Monte Rosa and the Matterhorn. The summit is reached from the Gandegg Hut via the Theodule Pass in about 4 hours, while a shorter (1½ hour) ascent of the south-west flank is often tackled from the Klein Matterhorn, graded PD-. The Breithorn is an extremely popular mountain, but given the serious nature of crevassed areas and the difficulties of route-finding in poor visibility, it should never be underestimated.

3: THE MATTERHORN: At 4477 metres this is possibly the one alpine peak all attracted to mountains would love to climb. The standard route by way of the Hörnli ridge is not difficult by alpine standards, but is nevertheless a serious undertaking for novices, the rock being loose and downright dangerous in places. (The route is graded AD-, with numerous individual grade II and III rock pitches.) One of the problems faced by climbers on this route is salvos of stonefall; another, general to this mountain, is the bad weather it attracts. From the Hörnli Hut an average time to the summit for experienced climbers would be 5–6 hours.

4: MONTE ROSA: Containing the second highest summit in the Alps (the 4634m Dufourspitze) the Monte Rosa massif, which has no less than ten 4000 metre tops, is the largest mountain mass in Western

Europe. Shared between Switzerland and Italy this beautiful snow- and ice-bound mountain boasts a number of lengthy routes. From the Monte Rosa Hut (see Appendix A) the Dufourspitze may be tackled by a popular snow climb up its north-west flank and then along the west ridge in 6–7 hours (PD, II+ 40°). The first ascent was achieved in August 1855.

There are, of course, numerous other peaks in the area, many of which have routes of greater interest or challenge to experienced climbers. In addition there are glacier tours that would provide memorable days out. You need never run short of ideas in Zermatt.

APPENDIX C:

Useful Addresses

1: Tourist Information:

Switzerland Tourism
Swiss Centre
Swiss Court
London W1V 8EE
☎ 020 7734 1921
stc@stlondon.com
www.myswitzerland.com

608 Fifth Avenue
New York
NY 10020
☎ 212 757 5944
stnewyork@switzerland
tourism.com

Canton Valais Tourist Office:
Valais Tourisme
Rue Pré-Fleuri 6
CH 1951 Sion
Switzerland
☎ (027) 327 35 70
info@valaistourism.ch
http://www.valaistourism.ch

Valais Rambling Association:
Association Valaisanne de la
   Randonnée Pédestre
Rue Pré-Fleuri 6
CH 1951 Sion
Switzerland
☎ (027) 327 35 80
info@valrando.ch

British Mountaineering Council
177–179 Burton Road
Manchester M20 2BB
☎ 0161 445 4747
office@thebmc.co.uk
www.thebmc.co.uk

Club Alpin Suisse
Monbijoustr. 61
3000 Bern 23
☎ (031) 370 18 18
info@sac-cas.ch
www.sac-cas.ch

2: Map Suppliers:

Edward Stanford Ltd
12 Long Acre
London WC2E 9LP
☎ 020 7836 1321
sales@stanfords.co.uk

The Map Shop
30a Belvoir St
Leicester
☎ 0116 247 1400

Rand McNally
444 N Michigan Ave
Chicago
Il 60611
☎ 312 321 1751

*(Rand McNally has 20+ stores
across the USA – for nearest store
(1 800 333 0136 – ext 211)*

3: Specialist Mountain Activities Insurance:

BMC Travel & Activity Insurance
(BMC members only)
177–179 Burton Road
Manchester M20 2BB
☎ 0161 445 4747
insure@thebmc.co.uk
www.thebmc.co.uk

Snowcard Insurance Services
Lower Boddington
Daventry
Northants NN11 6BR
☎ 01327 262805
orders@snowcard.co.uk
www.snowcard.co.uk

Austrian Alpine Club
2 Church Road
Welwyn Garden City
Herts AL8 6PT
☎ 01707 324835
manager@aacuk.demon.co.uk
info@hbinsurance.co.uk
aacuk.demon.co.uk
www.hbinsurance.co.uk

Harrison Beaumont Ltd
2 Des Roches Square
Witney
Oxon OX8 6BE
☎ 01993 700200

*(Membership of the AAC
carries accident & mountain rescue
insurance plus reciprocal rights
reductions in SAC huts.)*

APPENDIX D:

Bibliography

1: General Tourist Guides:

The Rough Guide to Switzerland by Matthew Teller (Rough Guides, London 2000) – Of the many general tourist guides on the market, this is the best and most comprehensive. Entertaining, factual, full of surprises and highly recommended.

Blue Guide to Switzerland by Ian Robertson (A&C Black, London) – Regularly updated and worth consulting.

Michelin Tourist Guide – French Alps (Michelin, Clermont-Ferrand 1998) – Useful information for visitors to the Chamonix–Mont Blanc region.

The Alps by R L G Irving (Batsford, London 1939) – Long out of print, but available on special request from public libraries (it may also be obtainable via internet booksearch sites), this book contains lengthy chapters on both the Mont Blanc range and that of the Pennine Alps, with some interesting background information.

2: Mountains & Mountaineering:

Numerous volumes devoted to mountaineering in regions of the Alps through which the Chamonix–Zermatt route travels are to be found in book-shops and libraries. Those listed below represent a very small selection, but there should be plenty of reading to provide an appetizer for a forthcoming visit – or to feed nostalgia.

The High Mountains of the Alps by Helmut Dumler and Willi P Burkhardt (Diadem Books, London/The Mountaineers, Seattle 1994) – A sumptuous large format book devoted to all the alpine 4000 metre peaks, of which there are many along the Haute Route. Mouth-watering photography and intelligent text make this a collector's item.

Alps 4000 by Martin Moran (David & Charles, Devon 1994) – This is the fascinating account of Moran's and Simon Jenkins's epic journey across all the 4000 metre summits of the Alps in one summer's frenetic activity.

Scrambles Amongst the Alps by Edward Whymper (first edition 1871, numerous editions since, including one published in 1986 by Webb & Bower, Exeter, with superb colour photos by John Cleare) – *Scrambles* is *the* classic volume of mountaineering literature which covers Whymper's alpine campaigns from 1860 to 1865. It contains the account of his fateful first ascent of the Matterhorn, but much more besides of interest to walkers of the Haute Route.

Wanderings Among the High Alps by Alfred Wills (Blackwell, Oxford – latest edition 1937) – Another record of Victorian adventures with guides on peaks and passes of the Pennine Alps, as well as other areas.

The Alps in 1864 by A W Moore (latest edition, Blackwell, Oxford 1939) – A two-volume personal account of a summer's mountaineering with Whymper and Horace Walker.

On High Hills by Geoffrey Winthrop Young (Methuen, London 1927) – Winthrop Young was one of the great pre-First World War climbers whose accounts are of high literary merit. This volume includes many references to the Pennine Alps.

Men and the Matterhorn by Gaston Rébuffet (Kaye & Ward, London 1973) – A well-illustrated book dedicated to the most famous mountain in Europe.

The Mountains of Switzerland by Herbert Maeder (George Allen & Unwin, London 1968) – Large format book with magnificent monochrome photographs.

The Outdoor Traveler's Guide to The Alps by Marcia R Lieberman (Stewart, Tabori & Chang, New York 1991) – Much of the range is covered, albeit in brief essays, but Mont Blanc and several of the Pennine valleys are treated well. The book is illustrated by Tim Thompson's high-quality colour photographs.

Alpine Ski Tour by Robin Fedden (Putnam, London 1956) – An account of the High Level Route ski traverse.

3: Mountain Walking:

The Valais by Kev Reynolds (Cicerone Press, Milnthorpe 1994) – A walking guide in the same series as the present book, it covers all the valleys of the Pennine Alps traversed on this route; 95 walks described.

Chamonix Mont Blanc by Martin Collins (Cicerone Press, Milnthorpe 1988) – A selection of walks in the shadow of Mont Blanc by a respected guidebook writer.

Tour of Mont Blanc by Andrew Harper (Cicerone Press, Milnthorpe 1988) – The early stages of the C–Z trek are shared by the TMB. This has long been the standard guide.

100 Hut Walks in the Alps by Kev Reynolds (Cicerone Press, Milnthorpe 2000) – As the title suggests, a large selection of alpine hut walks. Some of those used on the Chamonix–Zermatt route are included.

Classic Walks in the Alps by Kev Reynolds (Oxford Illustrated Press, Sparkford, 1991) – A large format book which describes, among others, the Chamonix–Zermatt route plus several day walks in the Pennine Alps.

Walking in the Alps by Kev Reynolds (Cicerone Press, Milnthorpe 1998) – From the Alpes Maritime to the Julians of Slovenia, 19 regions of the Alps are described with their walking and trekking potential in this 480 page hardback. The Pennine Alps and Mont Blanc range are well covered.

Walking in the Alps by J Hubert Walker (Oliver & Boyd, Edinburgh and London 1951) – Inspiration for the previous title, Walker's book has long been out of print. Although much has changed in the Alps since it was written, it remains one of the best and most readable of all alpine books. A fine chapter is devoted to the Pennine Alps.

Backpacking in the Alps and Pyrenees by Showell Styles (Gollancz, London 1976) – Contains an account of a large section of the Walker's Haute Route.

4: Climbing & Ski-touring Guides:

Valais East and *Valais West* by Lindsay Griffin (Alpine Club, London) – Produced by that doyen of mountaineering journalists, these two volumes condense and update a former three-volume series devoted to the Pennine Alps.

The Haute Route Chamonix–Zermatt by Peter Cliff (Cordee, Leicester) describes the glacier route for ski-tourers.

APPENDIX E:

Glossary

The following glossary is a selection of words likely to be found on maps, in village streets or in foreign-language tourist information leaflets. It is no substitute for a pocket dictionary, but hopefully will be of some practical use.

German	French	English
Abhang	pente	slope
Alp	haut pâturage	alp
Alpenblume	florealpe	alpine flower
Alpenverein	club alpin	alpine club
Alphütte	cabane, refuge	mountain hut
Auskunft	renseignements	information
Aussichtspunkt	belle vue	viewpoint
Bach	ruisseau	stream, river
Bäckerei	boulangerie	bakery
Bahnhof	la gare	railway station
Berg	montagne	mountain
Bergführer	guide de montagne	mountain guide
Berggasthaus	hotel en haut	mountain inn
Bergpass	col	pass
Bergschrund	rimaye	crevasse between glacier & rock wall
Bergsteiger	alpiniste	mountaineer
Bergwanderer	grimpeur	hillwalker
Bergweg	chemin de montagne	mountain path
Blatt	feuille	map sheet
Brücke	pont	bridge
Dorf	village	village
Drahtseilbahn	télépherique	cable-car
Ebene	plaine or plan	plain
Fels	rocher	rock wall
Ferienwohnung	apartement de vacances	holiday apartment
Fussweg	sentier, chemin	footpath

German	French	English
Garni	garni	b&b hotel
Gasthaus or gasthof	auberge	inn, guest house
Gaststube	salon	common room
Gefährlich	dangereaux	dangerous
Gemse	chamois	chamois
Geröllhalde	éboulis	scree
Gipfel	sommet, cime	summit, peak
Gletscher	glacier	glacier
Gletscherspalte	crevasse	crevasse
Gondelbahn	télécabin	gondola lift
Grat	arête	ridge
Grüetzi	bonjour	greetings
Jugendherberge	auberge de jeunesse	youth hostel
Kamm	crête	crest, ridge
Kapelle	chapelle	chapel
Karte	carte	map
Kirche	église	church
Klamm	gorge, ravin	gorge
Klumme	combe	combe, small valley
Landschaft	paysage	landscape
Lawine	avalanche	avalanche
Lebensmittel	épicerie	grocery
Leicht	facile	easy
Links	á gauche	left (direction)
Matratzenlager/ massenlager	dortoir	dormitory
Moräne	moraine	moraine
Murmeltier	marmot	marmot
Nebel	brouillard	fog, low cloud, mist
Nord	nord	north
Ober	dessus	upper
Ost	est	east
Pass	col	pass
Pension	pension	simple hotel
Pfad	sentier, chemin	path
Pickel	piolet	ice-axe

German	French	English
Quelle	source, fontaine	spring
Rechts	á droite	right (direction)
Reh	chevreuil	roe deer
Rucksack	sac à dos	rucksack
Sattel	selle	saddle, pass
Schlafraum	dortoir, chambre	bedroom
Schlafsaal	dortoir	dormitory
Schloss	château	castle
Schlucht	ravin, gorge	gorge
Schnee	neige	snow
See	lac	lake, tarn
Seil	corde	rope
Seilbahn	télépherique	cable-car
Sesselbahn	télésèige	chairlift
Stausee	réservoir	reservoir
Steigesen	crampons	crampons
Steinmann	cairn	cairn
Steinschlag	chute de pierres	stonefall
Stunde(n)	heure(s)	hour(s)
Sud	sud	south
Tal	vallée	valley
Tobel	ravin boisé	wooded ravine
Touristenlager	dortoir	dormitory, simple accommodation
Über	via, par-dessus	via, or over
Unfall	accident	accident
Unterkunft	logement	accommodation
Verkehrsverein	office du tourisme	tourist office
Wald	forêt, bois	forest
Wanderweg	sentier, chemin	footpath
Wasser	eau	water
Weide	pâturage	pasture
West	ouest	west
Wildbach	torrent	torrent
Zeltplatz	camping	campsite
Zimme	chambres	bedrooms
- frei		- vacancies

ROUTE SUMMARY

Route	Dist	Ht gain	Time	Page
Route	**Dist**	**Ht gain**	**Time**	**Page**
1. Chamonix–Argentière	9 km	214m	2 hrs	37
2. Argentière–Col de Balme–Trient	12 km	953m	5–5½ hrs	43
A2. Argentière–Col de Balme–Les Grands–Col de la Forclaz	15 km	953m	6½–7 hrs	49
3. Trient–Fenêtre d'Arpette–Champex	14 km	1386m	6½–7 hrs	52
A3. Trient–Col de la Forclaz–Bovine–Champex	16 km	876m	5½ hrs	58
4. Champex–Sembrancher–Le Châble	13 km	104m	3½–4 hrs	61
5. Le Châble–Clambin–Cabane du Mont Fort	9 km	1636m	6–6½ hrs	66
6. Cab. du Mont Fort–Col de Louvie–Col de Prafleuri–Cab. de Prafleuri	14 km	885m	6–6½ hrs	73
A6. Cab. du Mont Fort–Col de la Chaux–Col de Prafleuri–Cab. de Prafleuri	10 km	885m	5½ hrs	80
7. Cab. de Prafleuri–Col des Roux–Col de Riedmatten–Arolla	16 km	735m	6½ hrs	83
A7. Cab. de Prafleuri–Col des Roux–Cab. des Dix	11 km	797m	4–4½ hrs	91

Route	Dist	Ht gain	Time	Page
A7a. Cab. des Dix–Pas de Chèvres– Cab. des Aiguilles Rouges/Arolla	10 km	428m	4 hrs	94
	10 km	215m	4 hrs	97
8. Arolla–Lac Bleu–Les Haudères–La Sage	10 km	1617m	5–5½ hrs	103
9. La Sage–Col du Tsaté–Cabane de Moiry	10 km	1252m	5 hrs	109
A9. La Sage–Col de Torrent–Barrage de Moiry	14 km	455m	5–5½ hrs	113
10. Cabane de Moiry–Col de Sorebois–Zinal	8 km	591m	4–4½ hrs	118
A10. Barrage de Moiry–Col de Sorebois–Zinal	14 km	1199m	5½–6 hrs	121
11. Zinal–Forcletta–Gruben	10 km	725m	4 hrs	128
A11. Zinal–Hotel Weisshorn	9 km	589m	4 hrs	132
A11a. Hotel Weisshorn–Meidpass–Gruben	16 km	1072m	7½ hrs	136
12. Gruben–Augstbordpass–St Niklaus	4 km	532m	1½–2 hrs	145
12a. St Niklaus–Gasenried	18 km	479m	5½ hrs	149
A13. St Niklaus–Täsch–Zermatt	14 km	1031m	5½–6 hrs	155
13. Gasenried–Europa Hut	18 km	348m	6½–7 hrs	160
14. Europa Hut–Täschalp–Zermatt				

LISTING OF CICERONE GUIDES

NORTHERN ENGLAND
LONG DISTANCE TRAILS

THE DALES WAY
THE ISLE OF MAN COASTAL PATH
THE PENNINE WAY
THE ALTERNATIVE COAST TO COAST
NORTHERN COAST-TO-COAST WALK
THE RELATIVE HILLS OF BRITAIN
MOUNTAINS ENGLAND & WALES
    VOL 1 WALES. VOL 2 ENGLAND.

CYCLING

BORDER COUNTRY BIKE ROUTES
THE CHESHIRE CYCLE WAY
THE CUMBRIA CYCLE WAY
THE DANUBE CYCLE WAY
LANDS END TO JOHN O'GROATS
    CYCLE GUIDE
ON THE RUFFSTUFF -
    84 Bike Rides in Nth Engl'd
RURAL RIDES No.1 WEST SURREY
RURAL RIDES No.1 EAST SURREY
SOUTH LAKELAND CYCLE RIDES
THE WAY OF ST JAMES
    Le Puy to Santiago - Cyclist's

LAKE DISTRICT AND MORECAMBE BAY

CONISTON COPPER MINES
CUMBRIA WAY & ALLERDALE RAMBLE
THE CHRONICLES OF MILNTHORPE
THE EDEN WAY
FROM FELL AND FIELD
KENDAL - A SOCIAL HISTORY
A LAKE DISTRICT ANGLER''S GUIDE
LAKELAND TOWNS
LAKELAND VILLAGES
LAKELAND PANORAMAS
THE LOST RESORT?
SCRAMBLES IN THE LAKE DISTRICT
MORE SCRAMBLES IN THE
    LAKE DISTRICT
SHORT WALKS IN LAKELAND
    Book 1: SOUTH
    Book 2: NORTH
    Book 3: WEST
ROCKY RAMBLER'S WILD WALKS
RAIN OR SHINE
ROADS AND TRACKS OF THE
    LAKE DISTRICT
THE TARNS OF LAKELAND Vol 1: West
THE TARNS OF LAKELAND Vol 2: East
WALKING ROUND THE LAKES
WALKS SILVERDALE/ARNSIDE
WINTER CLIMBS IN LAKE DISTRICT

NORTH-WEST ENGLAND

WALKING IN CHESHIRE
FAMILY WALKS IN FOREST OF
    BOWLAND
WALKING IN THE FOREST OF
    BOWLAND
LANCASTER CANAL WALKS
WALKER'S GUIDE TO LANCASTER

CANAL
CANAL WALKS VOL 1: NORTH
WALKS FROM THE LEEDS-LIVERPOOL
    CANAL
THE RIBBLE WAY
WALKS IN RIBBLE COUNTRY
WALKING IN LANCASHIRE
WALKS ON THE WEST PENNINE
    MOORS
WALKS IN LANCASHIRE WITCH
    COUNTRY
HADRIAN'S WALL
    Vol 1 : The Wall Walk
    Vol 2 : Wall Country Walks

NORTH-EAST ENGLAND

NORTH YORKS MOORS
THE REIVER'S WAY
THE TEESDALE WAY
WALKING IN COUNTY DURHAM
WALKING IN THE NORTH PENNINES
WALKING IN NORTHUMBERLAND
WALKING IN THE WOLDS
WALKS IN THE NORTH YORK MOORS
    Books 1 and 2
WALKS IN THE YORKSHIRE DALES
    Books 1,2 and 3
WALKS IN DALES COUNTRY
WATERFALL WALKS - TEESDALE &
    HIGH PENNINES
THE YORKSHIRE DALES
YORKSHIRE DALES ANGLER'S GUIDE

THE PEAK DISTRICT

STAR FAMILY WALKS PEAK
    DISTRICT/Sth YORKS
HIGH PEAK WALKS
WEEKEND WALKS IN THE PEAK
    DISTRICT
WHITE PEAK WALKS
    Vol.1 Northern Dales
    Vol.2 Southern Dales
WHITE PEAK WAY
WALKING IN PEAKLAND
WALKING IN SHERWOOD FORES
WALKING IN STAFFORDSHIRE
THE VIKING WAY

WALES AND WELSH BORDERS

ANGLESEY COAST WALKS
ASCENT OF SNOWDON
THE BRECON BEACONS
CLWYD ROCK
HEREFORD & THE WYE VALLEY
HILLWALKING IN SNOWDONIA
HILLWALKING IN WALES Vol.1
HILLWALKING IN WALES Vol.2
LLEYN PENINSULA COASTAL PATH
WALKING OFFA'S DYKE PATH
THE PEMBROKESHIRE COASTAL PATH
THE RIDGES OF SNOWDONIA
SARN HELEN
SCRAMBLES IN SNOWDONIA
SEVERN WALKS

THE SHROPSHIRE HILLS
THE SHROPSHIRE WAY
SPIRIT PATHS OF WALES
WALKING DOWN THE WYE
A WELSH COAST TO COAST WALK
WELSH WINTER CLIMBS

THE MIDLANDS

CANAL WALKS VOL 2: MIDLANDS
THE COTSWOLD WAY
COTSWOLD WALKS Book 1: North
COTSWOLD WALKS Book 2: Central
COTSWOLD WALKS Book 3: South
THE GRAND UNION CANAL WALK
HEART OF ENGLAND WALKS
WALKING IN OXFORDSHIRE
WALKING IN WARWICKSHIRE
WALKING IN WORCESTERSHIRE
WEST MIDLANDS ROCK

SOUTH AND SOUTH-WEST ENGLAND

WALKING IN BEDFORDSHIRE
WALKING IN BUCKINGHAMSHIRE
CHANNEL ISLAND WALKS
CORNISH ROCK
WALKING IN CORNWALL
WALKING IN THE CHILTERNS
WALKING ON DARTMOOR
WALKING IN DEVON
WALKING IN DORSET
CANAL WALKS VOL 3: SOUTH
EXMOOR & THE QUANTOCKS
THE GREATER RIDGEWAY
WALKING IN HAMPSHIRE
THE ISLE OF WIGHT
THE KENNET & AVON WALK
THE LEA VALLEY WALK
LONDON THEME WALKS
THE NORTH DOWNS WAY
THE SOUTH DOWNS WAY
THE ISLES OF SCILLY
THE SOUTHERN COAST TO COAST
SOUTH WEST WAY
    Vol.1 Mineh'd to Penz.
    Vol.2 Penz. to Poole
WALKING IN SOMERSET
WALKING IN SUSSEX
THE THAMES PATH
TWO MOORS WAY
WALKS IN KENT Book 1
WALKS IN KENT Book 2
THE WEALDWAY & VANGUARD WAY

SCOTLAND

WALKING IN THE ISLE OF ARRAN
THE BORDER COUNTRY -
    A WALKERS GUIDE
BORDER COUNTRY CYCLE ROUTES
BORDER PUBS & INNS -
    A WALKERS' GUIDE
CAIRNGORMS, Winter Climbs
    5th Edition

LISTING OF CICERONE GUIDES

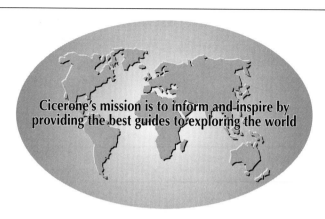

Since its foundation over 30 years ago, Cicerone has specialised in publishing guidebooks and has built a reputation for quality and reliability. It now publishes nearly 300 guides to the major destinations for outdoor enthusiasts, including Europe, UK and the rest of the world.

Written by leading and committed specialists, Cicerone guides are recognised as the most authoritative. They are full of information, maps and illustrations so that the user can plan and complete a successful and safe trip or expedition – be it a long face climb, a walk over Lakeland fells, an alpine traverse, a Himalayan trek or a ramble in the countryside.

With a thorough introduction to assist planning, clear diagrams, maps and colour photographs to illustrate the terrain and route, and accurate and detailed text, Cicerone guides are designed for ease of use and access to the information.

If the facts on the ground change, or there is any aspect of a guide that you think we can improve, we are always delighted to hear from you.

Cicerone Press
2 Police Square Milnthorpe Cumbria LA7 7PY
Tel:01539 562 069   Fax:01539 563 417
e-mail:info@cicerone.co.uk   web:www.cicerone.co.uk

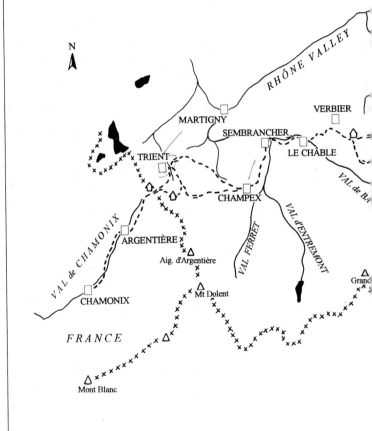

THE CHAMONIX-ZERMATT
WALKER'S HAUTE ROUTE

N

RHÔNE VALLEY

MARTIGNY

VERBIER

SEMBRANCHER

LE CHÂBLE

TRIENT

CHAMPEX

VAL de BA

VAL de CHAMONIX

ARGENTIÈRE

Aig. d'Argentière

VAL FERRET

VAL d'ENTREMONT

CHAMONIX

Grand

Mt Dolent

FRANCE

Mont Blanc